How to Grill a Gourmet

By Ivan Meursault

PROCTOR PUBLICATIONS, LLC

Proctor Publications, LLC
P.O. Box 2498 • Ann Arbor, Michigan 48106
800-343-3034
www.proctorpublications.com

PUBLISHER'S CATALOGING-IN-PUBLICATION
(Provided by Quality Books, Inc.)

Meursault, Ivan
    How to grill a gourmet / by Ivan Meursault. -- 1st
ed.
    p. cm.
    LCCN: 00 136220
    ISBN: 1-928623-03-4

    1. Restaurants--Fiction. 2. Cookery, French--
Fiction. 3. Gourmets--Fiction. I. Title.

PS3563.E853H69 2000   813'.6
                               QBI00-901792

INTRODUCTION

by

William J. Conlin

Here's a fact. Ninety percent of all new restaurants close within the first year. Now here's a lesser known fact. Ninety percent of those surviving the first year close within the first two weeks of the second year. *I know.* My restaurant, or rather *our* restaurant, lasted exactly one year and two weeks!

That's what this story is all about.

Nine well-intentioned, otherwise successful business and professional people, at my urging, decided to start a *really good French restaurant* in Ann Arbor, Michigan. As many Ann Arborites will remember, it was called *La Seine.* John Mersereau, Jr., the author of the story, has changed the name to *La Garonne,* choosing for himself the *nom de plume* of Ivan Meursault, reflecting his academic career in Russian literature and his love of the best French white burgundy. Why he calls me *Jack Corcoran* I don't know, except that the name might have suggested itself as being somewhat Irish and the *cork* part a clue to my avocational interests.

It all started very simply. One day in the spring of 1968, Judy Dow brought Gerry Meyers, then the manager of Weber's Inn Restaurant, to my office and told me he wanted to create a sophisticated dining establishment. I called around, and shortly had hooked nine acquaintances, and we began planning—and spending. Each of the assembled investors had had his own dining experiences at great restaurants at home and abroad, and our collective imaginations, fueled by the libations that accompanied our evening sessions, led inevitably, or so it seemed, to increasingly lavish visions of what we hoped to create. Our initial intention of a simple French bistro with checkered tablecloths and candles in wine bottles, somehow evolved, at least in our vision, into a second *Tour d'Argent.*

Remember, in 1968 there was only one *sort-of-gourmet* restaurant in Ann Arbor, *The Rubiyat.* And at that time Ann Arbor was virtually dry, a legacy of Prohibition. Liquor by the glass was the exception. If you wanted something more substantial than beer or wine, you had to belong to a club. That's why we bought *The Sugar Bowl* – it had a full-service liquor license.

Today Ann Arbor is the restaurant Mecca of the Midwest. Any magazine that concerns good food will mention our city. The entire downtown is one big food bazaar, with prices ranging from triple expensive to eminently affordable. Today you can go to a restaurant and spend $75 a person even before you know it. But at that time, *La Seine* entrées ranged from $6 - $10, and the *prix fixe* dinner was just $6.50. Admittedly, most people spent far beyond that. In fact, I met a friend on the street one day and he told me, "Bill, we were going to go to your restaurant last night but decided to buy a color TV instead."

Ruth Reichl, editor of *Gourmet Magazine*, worked as a waitress at *La Seine*, which she calls *L'Escargot* in her book *Tender At the Bone.* Her vision of our restaurant is substantially different from ours. Her description of what she calls *Show-off Salad* is perfect, but, as she admits, sometimes she ignores facts for the sake of a good story. She views the restaurant's demise as a result of "tote," that is the amazing capacity of chops, steaks, wine, and other beverages to walk out the back door—under someone's coat, of course. I agree we suffered pilferage of various degrees, but our downfall was the result of the owners naiveté and poor management.

Halfway through the year we had a substantial pile of bills from remodeling the building. One of our partners suggested that we somehow get rid of "the leeches." I instructed him that since they were businessmen who had extended us credit, the term "leeches" seemed ungracious. However, I said I would settle for his using "unfriendly creditors," a term which was not inappropriate. Some of our suppliers were, in fact, unaccountably hostile: when confronted by one particularly aggressive supplier, even I began to have fears of a cement overcoat.

Another annoyance was having to handle complaints. One Saturday night at 11:00 PM a well-known physician from the University Hospital called to inform me that he was at *La Seine* and his reservation was not being honored. He was angry and wanted me to do something about it. That was just one of the incidents which indicated that something was wrong with management.

Perhaps those readers who are old enough to remember *La Seine* can guess the identities of our investors. And others may still wonder if we went bankrupt. Not quite! Our lease had an option to buy, and when the restaurant closed, the building still remained in our possession. The bank next door, on the corner of Huron and Main, was experiencing growing pains and bought our property, thus providing enough (barely) to satisfy "those leeches." Location is everything!

Today there are many publications devoted to "How to do this or that." John's book is on "How Not to Run a Restaurant." But his account is full of hilarious episodes which today, from the distance of three decades, still provoke a lot of laughs. *At least he who laughs last . . . .*

How to

Grill

a

Gourmet

Ivan Meursault

1

The setting for this *comédie française* was a small university town named Huron, which called itself "the Athens of the Midwest," probably because it had so many Greek restaurants. These were disguised under a variety of names suggesting the cuisine of Bavaria, the Orient, Italy or other tasty locales, but that inevitable ochre sauce, which renders chicken indistinguishable from pork, betrayed their common heritage. Anyway, it was primarily from a surfeit of Southern Adriatic cooking that wistful hopes for a "really good" restaurant were expressed so often in and about Huron. Most people were content to keep their desires comfortably and safely on the plane of wishful thinking. Not so the nine little Indians, who seriously and, it must be said, not quite soberly determined to engage in the ultimate act of pretentious folly — to open a "really good" French restaurant.

Haute cuisine in Huron started to become a reality one steaming July afternoon in the office of a lawyer named Jack Corcoran, who, although still in his middle thirties, had an established reputation as expeditor, investor, and *bon-vivant*. He and I had known each other about ten years, ever since I had joined the local university, our close and continuing friendship challenging a prevalent myth that town and gown were mutually incompatible. On the afternoon in question, I was preparing to flee the stifling halls of Academe for the sylvan suffocation of the suburbs

1

when the phone caught me. Jack insisted I come down to his office right away, because, he promised, a deal was cooking which he thought might very likely intrigue me. He insinuated that both profit and pleasure were involved. I objected that the overheated asphalt downtown was more menacing than the La Brea tar pits, and besides that I had a date with a gin and tonic, but he persisted, mentioning in passing that the air conditioning in his new offices was functioning perfectly. The bait worked, and within five minutes I was being ushered into the luxurious chill of his paneled suite.

Jack was already balding, and only skillful tailoring screened the evidence that he was an overzealous admirer of his wife's culinary accomplishments. His unmistakably Irish face, almost always tanned from a rigorous schedule of fall, winter, spring, and summer vacations, was set off by sharp blue eyes and a ready smile. He laughed a lot and gave an initial impression of being very easygoing, but he had a mind like a guillotine, swift, sharp, and merciless, and a memory which approached total recall. As I walked in, he was his usual buoyant self.

"Hi, Ivan," he greeted me. "Would you believe that today I had absolutely the worst lunch in fifteen years? A real acidosis special. I'd sue *The Turino Bar and Grill* for assault with a deadly Blue Plate Special, except that lawyers cost too much. My ulcer feels like a sea anemone, and it's snapped up a whole roll of *Tums* with zero effect. Anyway, that's why I called. Someone's coming in who wants to start a gourmet restaurant — I thought you might want a piece of the action."

I was appalled, or at least tried to give that impression. "You thought what? Interested in a restaurant? You told me yourself that anyone who invested in a restaurant deserved involuntary commitment to the funny farm."

Jack brushed aside my objection. "This will be different. A French restaurant. *Escargot, soupe à l'onion.* A fellow named Dicky is dropping by in a few minutes to discuss it. He's had lots of experience but needs some backing to open a place of his own. So-and-so (he mentioned a local patroness of the arts) brought him by last week. She says Dicky has a real flair. Just imagine, a real French restaurant right here in Huron. And we'll have wine in carafes and checkered tablecloths and intimate atmosphere and the food will be sensational and . . . ."

His enthusiasm was beginning to feed on itself, which was a sure sign that he'd already made up his mind but was merely convincing himself a little more before announcing a decision. He had to be stopped, so I broke in. "What do you mean by 'We'll have wine in carafes and checkered tablecloths'? Who's this 'we' you're talking about? Not me, I hope."

The response was expected and typical. "Nonsense, I'm counting you in. Definitely. You're always talking about the rotten food around here, and now you have a chance to do something about it."

Jack had me there. Admittedly, one of my favorite hobby horses was the subject of the wretched local cuisine — but invest in a restaurant? I tried an evasion on practical terms. "It'll cost a mint. And you can't have a restaurant without a liquor license. Where'll you get that?"

My demurer was ignored.

"Don't worry about the license. I'll see to that. I've gotten licenses for lots of people, so don't think I can't get one for us."

I knew he was right, but I didn't dare concede anything. He was closing the net, and I was getting panicky.

"But restaurants always fail. You've said that for years."

My plaintive tone revealed my indecision, and Jack, I was horrified to see, had the look of a fisherman just about to land a whopper.

He proceeded, "This will be different. I'm not one for failures, and this can't fail because we'll be running it."

I thought I saw an escape.

"So, I suppose you'll give up your practice and I'll resign from the university and together we'll run this show? I can just see you leaving these new offices for some cubby hole next to a hot kitchen."

Jack made a face.

"Don't be silly. Dicky, the fellow who's coming in, will actually manage the operation, but we'll control it. We'll keep complete charge of all finances and set the policies."

I made one last desperate effort.

"Speaking of finances, where are we going to get the money? I don't have an extra cent, and you've been crying poor yourself in recent months."

He assumed the tone one uses when dealing with stubborn children.

"First, there'll be eight or ten of us in on the deal. If we each put up four thousand, that makes forty thousand to get started. That's more than enough, and we can get a line of credit at the bank for the rest. And to get your four thousand, you'll do just what I'm going to do, go across the street to the friendly bank and take out a personal loan."

Having disposed of that matter, his enthusiasm returned. "Just think of it. No more long trips to Metropolis just to get a decent dinner. We'll have it right here — tiny medallions of veal with shallots and truffles, real French onion soup, *patisserie*, good wines. There's no competition. It's bound to be the best idea of the year."

The seductive vision of a charming bistro with checkered tablecloths and candles dripping wax over musty bottles, the redolence of *sauce bordelaise*, the image of attentive waiters deftly manipulating fork and spoon captured my imagination and dulled the mundane considerations of money and risk. I felt myself weakening. At that juncture, Jack's secretary rang and announced that the "restaurant man" had arrived. She was told to show him in. Moments later he appeared, a somewhat gangly young fellow with a springy step and an indecisive, sort of naughty puppy grin. Jack waved him in and introduced us. I said something about the punitive nature of the weather, he agreed, and we sat down.

For my benefit, Jack ran quickly over the discussion which had taken place during his first meeting with Dicky. At that time, he had learned that Dicky had broad experience as waiter, captain, and *maître d'hotel* and that he was now ready to manage a place of his own. His hope was to create an intimate establishment with excellent food and service. Jack's suggestion that the restaurant have a French character had been fine with Dicky.

Our conversation was rather general. Dicky's characterization of the local restaurant scene showed perception (mediocre to terrible) and his enthusiastic expression of a commitment to good food, fine service, and congenial decor was convincing and infectious. He had studied the operation of the best restaurants in the state and, he stated, he could count on the friendly advice of several successful operators in Metropolis and elsewhere. In talking about the project with friends, he had found two who were especially anxious to become investors. He presumed that Jack would be able to find the others.

Jack anticipated no difficulties.

"We've got four already, Dicky, with your two and the professor here and myself. The others won't be hard to find. We'll have to beat them off when word of this gets around town. You just keep looking for a good location with a liquor license and I'll handle the purchase. Let me know when you've found something and we'll go on from there."

Dicky shortly took his leave, and I followed, somewhat perplexed at finding myself so suddenly involved in an enterprise so fraught with perils. But, after all, I told myself, Dicky seems to know what he's doing and four thousand dollars is a modest sum for part of a sure-fire winner. And what a change it would be to have a decent restaurant right in town, just minutes away. But there was also a captivating little concept germinating in my head that had nothing to do with either earnings or eating but lots to do with ego. I, Ivan Meursault, professor, author of scholarly books, world traveler, would now enhance my image through public recognition (albeit belated) of my attributes as gourmet and connoisseur. For certainly it was I who would set the standards for the cuisine of our establishment, it was I who would be consulted by an appreciative chef about his menus, it was I who would select (and taste) the wines for our outstanding cellar. I, Ivan Meursault, would be recognized and admired as epicure and . . .! Such heady thoughts naturally dispelled pedestrian considerations of financial risk, and by the time I had reached home I was eagerly committed to Jack's plan. In culinary terms, "my fat was in the fire."

2

Within two weeks, Jack had seeded the field and harvested a crop of investors, all possessed of some assets and gourmet aspirations — or pretensions. I had met all of them at one time or another, but I didn't know any of them very well. Dwight, a pleasant appearing, even tempered doctor in his thirties, seemed a good choice. He had an interest in wines, his wife had the reputation of a good cook, and it was known that he never passed up a good restaurant when travelling. It was also known that he was no stranger to success with various investments around Huron.

Dwight himself recruited his close friend Eric, a mercurial young manufacturer whose size and temperament would have guaranteed, had he lived in an earlier age, a brilliant career as Viking, knight, or buccaneer. Close acquaintance revealed that despite his rough-hewn features and ominous proportions, he had a ready sense of humor. As for his interest in our project, he was eager to purchase the best that kitchen and cellar could provide.

Ricardo, a matured European *homme d'affaires* with a command of Italian, French, and modern Greek, was a natural choice, his very presence adding a continental air to our group. Tall, thin, with aquiline features and jet black hair, he dressed impeccably and manifested the manners of an aristocrat, even to the kissing of ladies' hands. His interest in the finer things of life was well established, and this assured us of his devotion to our mutual cause.

Jack's final selection, Hughes, was also middle-aged, an entrepreneur of grave demeanor and ritualized formality. Conservatism in dress, behavior and politics were his hallmarks. He had a reputation for fiscal acuity, or, as someone once put it rather maliciously, "He would skin a gnat for its hide and tallow." Jack had chosen him as a modifying influence on his own tendencies to buy now and pay later.

The two friends that Dicky had promised to bring into the undertaking proved most congenial. Ralph was the older of the two, about forty-five, of medium height, with steel grey hair combed straight back, close to the scalp. He wore yellow tinted glasses and displayed an unchanging Cheshire grin. His attire bespoke a man with little concern for convention, for he favored modish jackets and cuffless checkered pants — quite a contrast to Ricardo's restrained sartorial elegance and Hughes' dark blue suits with vest. We had heard that Ralph owned several plants and that money was no problem for him, either to make it or spend it.

Dicky's other friend, Willis, appeared to be a typical young businessman, combining earnestness with boyish exuberance. He had an abundance of nervous energy and laughed constantly in a compulsive sort of way. Both he and Ralph had full confidence in Dicky and were eager to see him fulfill his potential as a restaurateur.

As for myself, the first to surrender to Jack's blandishments, I had just reached the age at which, according to the adage, life begins. My qualifications for this venture, as Jack outlined them for the edification of the other investors, were a command of café French, an exposure to European cuisine from San Francisco to Moscow, and the fact that my wife and I had once had an apartment on the Left Bank. Moreover, I was, notwithstanding my ten years' sojourn in Huron, from "out of town," a circumstance which usually grants one the status of an expert in all things.

Such was our group. Though of widely disparate backgrounds and occupations, we were strongly united by our missionary zeal to bring *haute cuisine* to the heathens of Huron, and we were all prepared and apparently able to put our money where our mouths were. We immediately launched into a schedule of frequent meetings.

The persistent heat that summer made iced drinks an absolute necessity at our gatherings, and these cool and calming potations caused us to believe that all we needed was a little time, a little capital, and our corporate brains — a distinguished restaurant would be the inevitable result. As luck would have it, at that time Dicky was conveniently free of professional obligations, so he could give full time to the project. We agreed that he would create the restaurant in the image we envisioned and serve as its manager. Some of Jack's recruits were a little concerned about Dicky's youth — he was the youngest of us all — and lack of actual managerial experience, but Ralph and Willis, who had known Dicky for years and were acquainted with his professional performance, assured the doubters that he had sufficient knowledge and was, in general, a fine fellow. As to his ability to create a luxury restaurant with striking decor, that was unquestioned in view of his "unusual creativity." Dicky himself was convincingly persuasive, and everyone was staunchly behind him after he promised that our restaurant would receive the coveted *Holiday Magazine* award within one year. As a gesture of confidence, we all agreed to co-sign a bank loan for him, so that he could hold shares of stock in the enterprise as an equal "partner."

Our dour entrepreneur, Hughes, agreed to work with Dicky as a sort of financial watchdog. This seemed an excellent combination, for Hughes' decorous middle age and regard for convention would, we all felt, have a salutary and modifying influence upon the possibly excessive enthusiasm of our youthful manager. And Hughes' business acumen would protect us from any fiscal inexperience on the part of our young colleague. We couldn't have wanted a better balanced team.

In the planning stages, we indulged not only our taste for scotch but enjoyed the pleasures of friendly disputation, arguing at length the pros and cons of table service with or without crests, the composition of a house salad dressing, the design of a canopy over the entrance, how best we might handle nationwide sales in volume of spices and sauces bearing our label, and whether it might not be slightly *gauche* to have our menu displayed in an illuminated frame outside the restaurant's doors.

An entire evening was devoted to the selection of the establishment's name, a subject fraught with personal preferences and prejudices. *Moulin Rouge* was howled down as suggestive of a bawdy atmosphere, *Le Petit Café* was rejected out of hand because semanticists among us were convinced that the adjective *petit* might give an impression of something less than the Lucullan feasts which would take place within. *Café de Paris* had a temporary following, but again it seemed inappropriate for the three-star establishment we had in mind. *Riems,* we felt, was difficult to pronounce and was subject to distortion to *rancid*. *Lyon* was discarded because the spelling might cause a delay in locating the number in the phone directory, although some believed this was a trivial objection. *Versailles* had real promise, and the image it simulated corresponded nicely with our own conception, but it was suggested too early in the evening to attract a majority. *Grenoble* lasted just long enough for someone to recall having had a bad meal in that city some fifteen years previously.

We turned to rivers, rapidly disposing of *Rhône*, *Dordogne*, *Moselle*, *Seine*, and *Loire*, finally reaching exhaustion of our geographic resources with *Garonne*. No one had anything positive to say, nor was there any particular opposition, so *La Garonne* it was. We parted with a pleasant sense of a job well done, the empties of *Cutty Sark* a witness to the intensity and duration of our efforts.

3

Dicky's search for an available restaurant ended at *The Coffee Spoon*, a Hellenic enterprise situated in the center of town which for many years had been owned and operated by a trio of brothers, who now wished to retire. Their establishment had one, and only one, positive asset, but that was indispensable for our purposes — a liquor license. According to the cruel and unusual laws governing the sale of alcoholic beverages in our state, the city of Huron was entitled to a limited number of licenses based on census figures, and all of these had been snapped up instantly only a few years earlier when the voters of Huron had finally decided that the Volstead Act was dead in fact and spirit. If *La Garonne* were to serve adult refreshment, we had to buy out a restaurant holding such a license. *The Coffee Spoon* was the only place with a license on the market at that time.

Preliminary explorations indicated that the old ark of a place might be converted to our purposes, and Jack began to discuss a lease-purchase deal with the brothers' lawyer. Soon an agreement in principle was reached, and all that remained was to put actual dollar figures into a contract. The brothers felt that such a delicate matter required their direct participation, so they invited Jack and any other available investors to meet at *The Coffee Spoon* to discuss the terms. The gathering was set at nine o'clock in the evening, when the restaurant's dinner clientele would have departed.

We began arriving at the appointed hour. Jack, ebullient as always, was obviously preparing to settle the brothers' hash with relish. In preparation for the negotiations, he had briefed Ricardo on a number of ploys and persuasions, and these he hoped would prove singularly effective when communicated by Ricardo in the brothers' native tongue. Hughes, our formal fiscal friend, arrived in a sombre mood befitting an occasion on which financial obligations are to be incurred. Dwight, Willis, and I had no assigned roles, other than to lend moral support and nod affirmatively or negatively on cue.

We were greeted cordially and ushered to a dark booth near the bar. Two of the brothers were present, and within a few minutes, assisted by a gaggle of relatives, they had cleared the surrounding tables of the remains of the "Dinner Special," meatloaf in ochre gravy with canned beans *Macedoine*. Once the evidence was removed, they joined us. Angelo was short, wiry, and loquacious, while Demo was large, lardy, and Sphinx-like. The third brother, Cosmo, never appeared, but he was there very much in spirit.

Angelo sensed our immediate anxiety and took steps to assuage it.

"How you guys lika little drinka? Now, whata you like, eh?"

We ordered. Then Jack, after suitably oiling his speech apparatus with several draughts of scotch and water, summarized the preliminaries he had discussed with the brothers' attorney. He proposed a fifteen year lease on the property with option to buy. We would cover all costs of remodeling, including any structural alterations called for by our design. As Jack began to detail some of the changes which Dicky's investigation had indicated might be necessary, Angelo's face acquired the expression of someone undergoing a tooth extraction.

"You no lika the place? You gonna mova the walls? You gonna taka somethin' out, maybe you never puta it back. Changa the name, OK, buta Cosmo he no lika you tear upa the place."

The opposition of the absent Cosmo had not been anticipated, but Jack rose to the challenge.

"Who said anything definite about moving walls? The restaurant's fine, just fine. But we have our own ideas, and some changes, mostly minor, will have to be made. Whatever we do, we'll do it right, count on that. Even Cosmo will approve."

"You gonna mova the walls, maybe you damage somethin' and who's gonna pay for that? Why don't you justa leava the walls? Sure, it'sa OK with me and Demo here, but Cosmo don'ta like. And if Cosmo don'ta like, you gotta no deal."

"Angelo, we'll take care of any damage. The lease will state that we are responsible, but at the same time we get to do what we want inside and out. Nothing will cost you a cent. We're going to put in air-conditioning, and that improves the value of your building. We'll add lounges and lights and carpeting, all of which make the property worth more. You can't complain about that."

"Wella, justa so it saysa that in the lease, so we gotta somethin' to showa to Cosmo, eh? Now, on the renta, our lawyer saysa you boys will paya twelve hundred dollar a month and alla utilities. That'sa too little, but we gotta retire and that'sa better than nothin'."

Jack wasn't playing that game. "Angelo, I love you like a brother, but I can't afford to talk with you because you cost me too much money. We offered six fifty a month, and I know *you* know that. The utilities we'll pay, but if you want to talk twelve hundred, you can talk to someone else."

"Now, notta so fast. Everythin's gonna be OK. Cosmo says twelve hundred and we gotta listen to him, 'cause he'sa the oldest. You knowa six fifty isa no good, is notta for us."

Jack gave a pained look. "Well, Cosmo better start liking something pretty soon or you'll be serving meatloaf here for longer than you think." He turned to Ricardo with a shrug, "Your turn."

Ricardo lightly fingered his silk tie, adjusted his gold stick pin, and then leaning his tall frame forward over the table, he launched into a passionate address to Angelo and Demo. His rich syllables apparently formed convincing words, for when he finished Angelo assumed an expression of resignation.

"Wella, Ricardo's an olda friend, and I trusta him to tella me straight. He saysa you boys can'ta go twelve hundred a montha for rent, so we're gonna maka it easy ona you. Cosmo won'ta like, but thisa time he's gotta to like. So let'sa say nine fifty and have a drink on it."

Jack's response was instantaneous. "Yes, let's have a drink, because we're just about to leave. Look, Angelo, we're renting this as a restaurant, not an office building. And we've got to re-model, which you know. And we pay the utilities, which most landlords have to pay. What's it cost a month to heat this place?"

"Wella, notta much. We gotta gooda furnace, and these older buildings was mada right, notta lika today. Now you knowa my cousin, he justa built *The Meteor Bar and Grill*, he paysa twice for heata whata we pay, and his place isa smaller. That'sa new building for you."

Jack forestalled further information about *The Meteor Bar and Grill* by interrupting. "Never mind. Look, we want this building, but at a fair price. We're a long way apart. I've told the other investors we would go seven fifty at most, if we had to." He looked at the rest of us for confirmation, and we nodded seriously. "I can't go more than that unless we have another directors' meeting."

"Now boys, you gonna getta this restaurant and atta nicea fair price. If we wasa younger, you couldn'ta geta it for fifteen hundred. But we gotta retire. We gotta fifty years worka behind us. We're gonna resta for a while, maybe travel somewhere, go to Florida in winter, see the old country. So we'ra ready to talka business."

Angelo beamed at us.

Jack's response was an imperative "Ricardo!" And Ricardo instantly took off on a rhetorical flight, his hands moving with a sculptor's grace as he caressed the ideas he sought to implant in the minds of the brothers. His words, though seemingly sweet, must have contained a bitter message, for when he finished Angelo responded with a vehement tirade, out of whose incomprehensible sounds popped an occasional *goddammit* and *sonofabitch*. The inscrutable Demo now entered the discussion, and the three of them carried on for a number of minutes, Angelo apparently hopping mad, Demo more sullen than angry, and Ricardo urbane as ever. Jack began to fidget and then interrupted.

"We can't spend all night. I'll take the responsibility on myself and go beyond the directors' authorization. We'll go to eight hundred a month. And bring me a last scotch, because I've got to go now. Is it settled?"

Angelo and Demo nodded unhappy acquiescence. Hughes, who had followed the deliberations with great intensity, remarked that in his opinion seven fifty was too much, but no one paid much attention. All of us were relieved that the matter was resolved, and although the lease was higher than we had hoped, the difference was only a drop in the bucket in terms of our projected weekly gross of $10,000 or more. Angelo distributed "one for the road" and sat down facing us.

"Now, boys, we gotta talka price for the business, the equipment, the liquora license."

Some of us did a double take. I, for one, had completely forgotten, owing to the length and intensity of the previous negotiations, not to mention marination in scotch, that the purchase of the business and the license was a matter separate from the lease. Angelo ignored our surprise.

"You can'ta getta the license excepta you buya the business, that'sa the law." He paused to emphasize the importance of legalities. "We gotta gooda business here, it'sa wortha gooda money. You getta all equipment, deep fries, soda fountain, icea cream machine, plates, everythin' isa here, you get. You getta business that'sa over fifty yearsa old, and you getta the gooda will. You getta all this and the liquora license for justa sixty thousand dollar. Believea me, that'sa gift."

We collectively flinched. Sixty thousand was a hell of a lot, especially as the equipment and furnishings had hardly any value for us. *La Garonne* could not conceivably use the soda fountain, and all the plates said *"Coffee Spoon"* on the rims. Further, it was entirely problematical whether the good will accrued from fifty years of serving meatloaf was transferrable to an establishment specializing in *haute cuisine*. But the brothers knew their strong suit, and if we wanted the license, we would have to take the junk with it. Jack countered with an offer of $20,000, the estimated worth of the license. And it went on from there, Ricardo increasingly called upon to break impasses in the negotiations.

More drinks, and finally a compromise at $45,000, payable at $250 a month, interest at 7%.

It was 2:00 A.M., and we were all emotionally exhausted and spiritually diluted. We shook hands on the deal to the accompaniment of some harridan's random imprecations as she rocked back and forth on a creaking bar stool in the dim recesses of the restaurant.

4

The place we had leased was reminiscent of the original ocean liner *Normandie* — after the fire. In the early thirties, *The Coffee Spoon* had been redone, but what was "keen" then was hardly "cool" almost four decades later. There were booths, whose cushions had committed *hara kiri*, varnished plaques along the walls to suggest paneling, and foggy mirrors. The floors were of those tiny white hexagonal tiles that nowadays are found only in subway lavatories and seedy theatres. The lighting was vintage neon, dead in some places, fluttering in others, and shatteringly bright in the dining areas. The furnishings were permeated with the smell of over half a century of Blue Plate Specials.

All this was clearly evident to the casual observer. Behind the scenes, in the kitchen, basement, and second floor, the situation was much worse, and those with the fortitude to prowl in those areas did so at considerable risk. This I was to learn a couple of days after our leasing session, when Jack insisted that Ricardo and I tour the place with him — we were supposedly knowledgeable about matters of plumbing, wiring, supports, and so forth. Jack and I met at his office and we made the brief walk to *The Coffee Spoon*, where we were shortly joined by our continental friend, resplendent in a camel's hair sport jacket and tapered trousers. As we proceeded through the abandoned kitchen, which reeked of leaking gas and odors best described as "Near

Eastern," Jack prepared us for what waited below and above.

"Don't expect carpeted floors. This is an old building and some of the basement is a little rough. But it's solid; is it ever solid. You should see the oak beams, all hand hewn. Watch out, these stairs are a little steep."

He flicked on a flashlight to illuminate the ladder and, like Virgil conducting Dante, led us downward into the gloom of the basement. After our eyes had adjusted somewhat to the darkness, we could see that we had reached the seventh circle. We were in a catacombs, and one could sense the presence of four and six-legged creatures just beyond the random patches of feeble light provided by bulbs on dropcords. Ricardo had smeared something on his sleeve while descending the stairs and was now trying to wipe it off. His first comment was a little rueful.

"Jack, but you should have told me it was so dirty. I would have worn my raincoat. This damp lime may ruin my jacket."

Such personal problems were intolerable to our guide, and he ignored the complaint.

"Right here at the foot of these stairs we'll have the store-room. Dicky has it all worked out. Just follow me down this way, because I want to show you the offices. Rather, where the offices will be. We'll have one for the chef and one for the manager, with a sliding window in between. Watch your head!"

The admonition came too late for the tall Ricardo, who now pressed his elegant handkerchief to his forehead and muttered something in Italian. In response to Ricardo's request to keep the light up, Jack explored the darkness overhead with his flashlight, revealing pipes of all dimensions running in every direction. The one that had attacked Ricardo had an aneurism which threatened him with imminent scalding or drowning. We quickly moved out of the danger area.

"What about the wiring?" I asked Jack. "There must be some lines other than just for the dropcords."

He swung his light along the walls and ceiling. Indeed there was wiring, a random webbing which disappeared through the ceiling and walls never to reappear. Obviously it would defy tracing. Ricardo's observation was hardly encouraging.

"Good lord, Jack, none of this will pass code. There's a violation every foot."

Jack was disappointed. We weren't reacting with the enthusiasm he had anticipated. In fact, I had an almost irresistible urge to flee before something dire happened. The place gave me the creeps, and the rough stone walls and tunnel-like openings seemed naturally to harbor giant mutated ants or, more likely, roaches. While these thoughts occupied my mind, our guide jauntily led us down an oozing stone corridor to a pitch black alcove. Strange tapping noises and mysterious snatches of sound intensified the horror.

"We're right under the front sidewalk," Jack announced. "This is the spot for our wine cellar. It's cool here and relatively dry. Dicky has planned to whitewash the stone and bricks and put racks for the wine bottles along the walls. For the moment that's all we'll do. But later, we'll have a circular staircase coming down over there from the foyer, and we'll sell wine retail. Our license includes sale of beer and wine over the counter."

Ricardo, hunched over to avoid further injury to his head, mentioned that the ceiling seemed awfully low, but Jack said that if necessary we could simply cut out the concrete floor and lower it. I kept silent, but I could just see someone cutting loose in there with an air hammer. Hand hewn oak beams or not, it seemed certain the old building would tumble in like a house of cards.

Having shown us the wine cellar, Jack permitted us to escape back to the kitchen. The bright lights there revealed that some destructive chemical reaction was taking place on the lime covered sleeve of Ricardo's jacket. He wasn't very happy about it. But the tour was not over yet. From in back of the bar we had to climb a real ladder into the inky black of the second floor, which was completely unlit except for Jack's flashlight. This part of the building had once been a candy factory, and the labyrinth of rooms was cluttered with sagging sinks, rotund coal stoves, and grotesque iron machines with hand cranks which once pulled taffy and churned chocolate. Jack had no particular plans for either the space or the machinery, so we stayed just long enough to satisfy our curiosity with regard to the confectionery museum pieces. Then down the ladder and back to the reeking kitchen, from which we departed up a long flight of canted stairs to the other section of the second floor. Here Jack's zeal did begin to make sense, for when he opened a door off the landing we saw a huge bare room whose distant windows looked out over the street.

"This will be for banquets," we were told. "There's no end of space, and Dicky has some other ideas as well. Maybe we'll cut out the center of the floor and make the place into a gallery over the main dining room. With tables along the railing, it would be sensational."

Ricardo asked a pertinent question.

"Is the floor strong enough to support a crowd?"

He jumped up and down lightly. It seemed quite solid. Jack answered from family history.

"My grandparents used to dance up here when it was a lodge hall. Of course it's strong enough. They used to have several hundred people up here."

That settled, he began to improvise other plans for using the space, all feasible and all, if implemented, profitable, such as an exclusive private club, a shop selling gourmet foods, a boutique specializing in French imports, or a cabaret with atmosphere *à la Toulouse Lautrec's* posters. Ricardo forgot his dissolving sleeve and entered into the mood of make-believe.

"And why not some small, intimate dining rooms, just for two, what we call in France *chambres separées.* Sometimes it is pleasant to dine in isolation, so that no one knows that you are present in the restaurant or who is your companion. These things are known in Europe." His dark eyes flashed with reminiscences.

Well, there was no denying that the old dance hall compensated with potential for what the basement presented in actuality. We ended our tour in a mood of positive thinking which repaid Jack for his efforts as guide.

5

The transformation of *The Coffee Spoon* to *La Garonne* began one torrid week in late summer under the general supervision of Dicky, who attacked the dilapidated decor and ancient equipment with unflagging dedication and energy. Within days, he had enlisted a small army of assistants, most of whom, we were told, were eager to volunteer their services in exchange for employment when the restaurant opened. Without regard for life or limb, and often in danger of electrocution or being buried alive, they tore out interior walls, smashed down sagging ceilings, and dragged trainloads of rubbish to trucks waiting in the back alley.

Meanwhile, a master plan for the furnishings and color scheme was being prepared by Micky, an aesthetic friend of Dicky's, whose sensitivities as an interior decorator had long been frustrated by the reactionary tastes of Huron's matrons. Micky wanted no fee, just an opportunity to express himself freely and creatively on the plastic and visual levels. We welcomed his services, particularly as they were *gratis*, and we silently commended Dicky for acquiring the collaboration of a professional at no cost to us.

Once the gutting was completed and the interior arrangement defined by newly erected walls, specialists were engaged to handle the more technical aspects of the reconstruction. The streets for blocks around the site seethed with panel trucks and pickups of artisans who installed plumbing, wiring, fire extinguishing systems, exhaust fans, air conditioners, furnaces and ice machines, and these were joined by the station wagons of contractors and vans of specialists who repaired compressors, recharged refrigeration lines, soldered steam tables, rebuilt dishwashers, checked and regulated thermostats, and put in locks. Because we didn't want to wait forever for the grand opening, many of these people worked overtime. The additional cost didn't particularly bother us, because our original estimate for all improvements had been a mere $15,000. Even at the time, we had all suspected that the renovation would be a little more than that.

Rumors as to the eventual character of the restaurant had circulated twice over. Some predicted a bistro, others a *Tour d'Argent*, and we investors were unable to confirm either, being far from certain ourselves what would be dictated by Micky and Dicky or necessitated by the trembling floors, the grinning wires, or the Minoan plumbing. A high plywood fence along the sidewalk prevented the curious from watching the operation that transformed the weather eroded face of *The Coffee Spoon* into the Gallic visage of *La Garonne*. Outside, a large sign merely announced that this was to be the future home of *Cuisine Classique Française* and that *Diner* and *Dejeunér* would be offered (the accent on *Déjeuner* had unaccountably floated from the first "e" to the last).

There was opposition, because Huron, like most small towns, believed in progress but disliked growing pains. The unceremonious removal of the old *Coffee Spoon's* sagging marquee from its precarious toehold of decades was protested as the desecration of a historical landmark. The application of a browny-citron paint to the whole exterior of the building stimulated a letter from the Main Street Merchants' Association expressing un-happiness. Actually, the color was hardly offensive in daylight, but at night, under the town's new mercury vapor lighting, it took on a bilious hue which instantly caused sensations of a stormy sea voyage. The new facade of vertically placed, rough-sawn boards, set off by a series of shallow arches on either side of mahogany doors, was received with reservations. Comment was not entirely favorable, either, when boxes of evergreens, sculpted like pom-poms, were placed before the arches.

Inside, safely hidden from the eyes of the public, a sensa-tional transformation was taking place under Micky's direction. In concrete terms, the creative urge our *gratis* interior decorator manifested itself in an orgy of expenditures, in which he enjoyed Dicky's full cooperation. New crystal chandeliers, naturally im-ported, rivaled those of *Maxim's*, the flocked burgundy wallpa-per was reminiscent of New Orlean's most elegant sporting house, the copper covered bar with a red velvet elbow cushion was unrivalled anywhere in the Midwest, and above it hung a sterling silver chandelier, opulently set in a tent of velveteen folds stretch-ing downwards to the rim of the canopy which overhung the bar. Sterling sconces enhanced the cocktail lounge's mahogany panel-ing, which had but recently graced the library of a rich estate, and baroque marble and bronze ornaments added additional dignity to the mantle of a false fireplace. Throughout stretched deep red carpeting, accented by velvet drapes whose texture was charac-terized by Micky as "gutsy". The ladies' and men's lounges were quietly elegant, with tasteful marble washstands and gleaming machines which dispensed paper-thin sheets of scented soap. On the gentlemen's side, the thoughtful Micky had made provision for displaying the daily issue of *The Wall Street Journal* over the urinals.

The word "economy" and its concept simply did not exist for Micky and Dicky, and our financial watchdog, Hughes, was completely ignored by this dynamic duo. If he withheld approval of a certain purchase, they would frustrate his veto by buying on credit. And if credit wasn't available, they would then take their case to the other owners, among whom there was a faction, headed by Jack, who felt that once we had found ourselves led down the velveted and chandeliered pathway, there was no point in going just half way. But Micky and Dicky were also very clever in not bringing up the matter of any controversial purchases until enough scotch had flowed to float their project to success. The matter of the glassware was typical.

The meeting that particular evening had followed the usual format: the secretary read the minutes of the previous session, Hughes requested and received approval for additional capitalization to the tune of several thousand dollars apiece, and Dicky provided explanations for not carrying out decisions adopted on prior occasions. He then gave us a pep talk about the cornucopia of profits we might expect the moment we opened our doors. This last pitch always put us in a cooperative mood.

That done, we got on with the aesthetics. Micky and Dicky had brought with them a mysterious box, from which they now produced a vast array of carefully wrapped objects. With obvious concern for suspense, Micky slowly and reverently unveiled the first item, revealing a delicate goblet, unmistakably crystal. Fingering the slender stem carefully, he informed us:

"These will be our burgundy glasses. They are unique, except for New York's most exclusive restaurant. With the silver and service plates, the effect will be exquisite."

Dwight, the tactful doctor, posed the question gently. "Aren't they a little fragile for a restaurant?"

Micky raised an eyebrow and looked meaningfully at Dicky.

"Well, we can hardly put our fine imported wines into nasty thick tumblers."

The doctor was properly chastened. He tried a conciliatory query.

"How much are they a dozen?"

"We have a special price just to us. And we don't have to pay anything down until the opening. Aren't they just exquisite?"

"Yes, but how much are they?"

"Dicky and I think they're very reasonable."

"Great! Order me four dozen for home."

"Well, they're a special order and it may take some time. But just give me a check for ninety-six dollars and I'll take care of it."

"My God, you mean two dollars each?"

"Well, even if they are, they're just too exquisite and we can't do without them. Besides, it's too late to cancel the order."

We were shown bordeaux glasses, champagne glasses, and every conceivable kind of bar glass, all crystal, all well over a dollar each, and all ordered in quantity. Micky pedantically informed us this would save money. The stem of the burgundy glass unaccountably snapped as they gently repacked it in the carton.

In the same way, they sold us on service plates which resembled antique pewter, with eroded crests that suggested they had been recovered from a sunken galleon — and as far as cost went, they might as well have been. The original idea of candles in wax-covered bottles was rejected as vulgar. Instead, we had tiny table lamps, whose inordinately expensive bulbs had a life-span slightly longer than a flashbulb. Those who provided these items conveniently arranged painless time payments. The renovations and furnishings, we were to learn later, added up to a trifling $100,000 — just five times the amount originally budgeted.

6

With the happy thought of the forthcoming opening, we gave consideration to the question of entertainment for that affair. The more conservative investors, with Hughes a country mile in the lead, expressed hope that our cuisine would be sufficient by itself, not to mention the luxurious decor and opulent table service. But Jack insisted that the initial image must be enhanced by the presence of a personality, a figure of international reputation whose mere name would connote all that epitomized France, gay elegance, *savoir faire*. The premiere of *La Garonne* should and would rival the best efforts of Hollywood or Broadway. As he warmed to his theme, spurred on by the fact that Hughes' gloom index was rapidly approaching 100%, he created a vision of Huron's brilliantly illuminated Main Street thronged with the curious as convoys of limousines deposited celebrities at our doorstep. The very least we would expect from the French government was the presence of a minister plenipotentiary, but likely the ambassador himself would be attracted by the lavishness of the affair. Maybe we should get the entire troupe from the *Lido* or the *Folies Bergère*, or . . .

At this point Hughes, who was wearing his "Jack's-at-it-again" look, declared that if Jack wanted an extravaganza, he would have to pay for it himself.

The retort was playful but pointed.

"Cheap, cheap, cheap. All right, why not? Who'll go in with me? We'll each put up a couple of hundred and get someone special, someone everyone knows, like Charles Trenet."

"Who," someone asked, "is Charles Trenet?"

Jack ignored the query. "Better yet, why not Maurice Chevalier? He's the real epitome of France. Not to do a program, but just to stroll around, sing a few songs, talk with the guests and add atmosphere. That's worth a couple of hundred to me. Who's game?"

I heard myself say "Sure," and Dwight also voiced approval. The modish Ralph, grinning from behind his tinted glasses, declared "Count me in." Eric suddenly jumped up, his bright face indicating that he had just been inspired by a happy thought. We turned to him expectantly.

"Jack, I'll even go five hundred for a celebrity, but only if she, and I repeat she, is someone like Brigitte Bardot. She can stroll around my table all she wants. She can even sit in my lap."

Hughes didn't know whether to take this seriously or not, but he did have a counter proposal.

"If you all have five hundred dollars for this kind of whim, may I suggest you save it for the air-conditioner. Our line of credit is exhausted, and we still have to buy some major pieces of equipment. You gentlemen don't seem to realize the obvious."

Jack was annoyed that Hughes was ruining the effects of his derring-do. He turned to our disapproving financial watchdog.

"Hughes, that's fine, we appreciate your concern about paying for the air-conditioner. But why can't we also have our grand opening? How many restaurants do you think you'll open in your lifetime? Just this once, can't we indulge ourselves a little?"

Hughes was incredulous. "Just this once? I frankly fail to understand your point of view." He became ironic. "Now, of course, we can always make some more personal contributions of cash and we can always extend the line of credit, and we can get deeper and deeper . . ."

Jack cut him short. "Hughes, I said I'd personally contribute my own money for this. The others can do the same if they like. We're not going to use corporation funds, although there's no real reason why we shouldn't. The presence of a celebrity at our opening will more than compensate for the expense. The advertising value alone is terrific. You can't buy publicity like what we'll get if Maurice Chevalier appears. And it has to be Chevalier, not Bardot," he addressed Eric, "because the good ladies of Huron would probably picket us if she appeared, and your wife, and my wife, and all of our wives would skin us alive if we paid to have her show up."

At this point, Ricardo's Mediterranean temperament got the better of his common sense and he joined the spendthrifts. The earnest young Willis, who had the expression of a Boy Scout in a no-limit poker game with hundred dollar chips, now manfully nodded his support. Eric acquiesced, and so Jack had his blank check.

The following morning, he contacted the epitome of France's agent in New York and experienced sudden sanity. The fee quoted for a weekend was $9,000. But Jack found humor even in his disappointment. When I lunched with him the next day, he found the whole episode amusing.

"We can't have the best, so let's have nothing at all. Anyway, it'll make Hughes happy. Think of the money we'll save.

You know me, cheap, cheap, cheap."

The unexpected economy in the area of entertainment made us all feel less restrained with regard to the cost of creating our distinguished wine cellar. Also, wines have a great potential for profit, so the more we invested at the outset, the more profit we would make later on. Once again, Dicky was assisted by some friendly experts who were happy to advise him in the matter, and in the weeks preceding the opening, the selections which they made began to arrive. We had *vin ordinaire* which turned out to be so ordinary as to be unpotable, and we had the finest, including a *Romanée Conti*. The *carte de vins* was itself a joy to behold, a handsome volume of red leather with illuminated pages carefully protected by transparent plastic covers. Merely to leaf through this document of elegance was to tour the famous chateaux of Bordeaux, to travel the length of *la Côte de Nuits* and *la Côte de Beane*. Other pages carried one to Anjou, to the Moselle region, to Alsace and Champagne. There was a generous choice of Italian and German wines, and those of the New World as well. The true connoisseur could hardly have wanted a greater variety from which to choose, except, as we were to learn, he could have wanted, and did want, vintages of better years and corks which weren't mouldy. We were also to learn, under less than amiable circumstances, that many of our finest labels were "on the verge" or even "over the hill."

7

The true French restaurant must have a French speaking staff. Besides providing the proper atmosphere, French speaking people instinctively know how to prepare and serve French food. So we thought. A committee, consisting of Jack, Ricardo, Dicky, and myself undertook to locate and hire the staff which was destined to put *La Garonne* on the culinary map. In a manner of speaking, we succeeded.

The chef rated first priority, so enticing advertisements were placed in Canadian and American French-language newspapers promising idyllic working conditions with generous salary and fringe benefits for a creative master of *haute cuisine*. Eagerly we awaited responses from aspiring Escoffiers, but none replied. Then out of the blue, and out of a job, materialized a Yugoslav, recommended by the man who had sold us our special-order china. In an excess of excitement, the committee scheduled its interview to coincide with the next meeting. That way, everyone would get a chance to see our candidate and form an opinion.

We met, as was our wont, at the home of one of the investors. That night our host was Ralph, who greeted us with his usual grin as we arrived at his ultramodern home. There was a bountiful offering of tasty snacks and a wide choice of drinks, the better to complement the pleasure we anticipated from the forthcoming interview. The prospective chef was not to appear until later, so we had our usual business meeting. Dicky presented a progress report which indicated a further postponement of the opening, and we bore up courageously under Hughes' typically doleful assessment of our financial posture. The formal meeting was adjourned at the second round of drinks, and this coincided with the arrival of the china salesman and the chef.

The Yugoslav proved most prepossessing and knowledgeable, discoursing freely and with an engaging European accent on his finesse with *ris de veau* and *coq au vin*. Hughes questioned him closely about the relationship between food costs and profits, and he assured us that he could coin money in our kitchen. The history of his previous employment was less encouraging, since none of us had ever heard of the "eggsellent" establishments which had profited from his association. But, of course, we all nodded solemnly when he mentioned the names of these places. We talked a bit more about our plans, fired by his enthusiasm and our own anticipation of particular dishes which this genius would prepare. But slowly the fact became apparent that the Yugoslav's diction was laboring under more than the problems of English pronunciation. In fact, not only was his speech slurring, but he was assuming a walleyed look which we had not observed on his arrival. Indeed, he was totally drunk, which Jack, with great hilarity, communicated to the unperceptive in a stage whisper audible to everyone except our handicapped chef. That unfortunate gent then confirmed the diagnosis by waving his empty glass at Ralph and demanding "Mohr trink!" Ultimately he was assisted out the door and poured into the back seat of the china salesman's car. Eric summed it up nicely: "That Yugoslav sure has a long tongue."

A few days after this depressing exhibition of human frailty, there was a heartening development in the form of a response to our advertisement from the wilds of Quebec Province. The correspondent, a Monsieur Renault, informed us that he was fully qualified as chef of a first-class restaurant, a fact attested by numerous diplomas and certificates from recognized institutes in France. He was seeking to further his art and reputation under favorable circumstances and was prepared to leave Canada to do so. He suggested an interview at his permanent residence in Quebec City.

The committee immediately detailed Dicky to fly there, which he did at once. In fact, he got there so soon that Monsieur Renault himself had not arrived from his place of employment in the hinterland. However, Dicky was able to find out many things about Monsieur Renault's qualifications from a certain Mademoiselle Louise, a lady of considerable, albeit faded, charms who fortuitously was at Renault's apartment when Dicky arrived. She provided a glowing description of the genius of this true, but hitherto insufficiently recognized, master. Her praise was so lavish that Dicky forthwith suggested that Monsieur Renault fly to Huron at our expense to talk with the entire committee, the journey also providing him an opportunity to inspect his prospective place of employment. This was entirely satisfactory, except that Mademoiselle Louise insisted she would have to accompany him. Monsieur Renault, she informed Dicky, did not speak English well enough to trust his own understanding of any financial particulars we might propose, and she was certain he would not accept any offer if she were not present to provide a complete and reliable translation. So two tickets were ordered.

Monsieur Renault and his companion arrived in Huron within a few days and were given a genial welcome by the members of the committee, Ricardo greeting them in fluent French while the rest of us muttered nasal sounds intended to represent French compliments and expressions of *fraternité*. Our man was short, plump, moustached, and otherwise a typical bourgeois, even to the calculation in his steely blue eyes. Everything we asked, dutifully translated by Mademoiselle Louise, was answered affirmatively, other than our request to peek at his diplomas. Through an oversight, these had been left in Quebec. Our offer of $225 a week was accepted without either enthusiasm or disappointment, after which he launched into a lengthy and rapid-fire address to his interpretress. She presented an abridged version: Monsieur Renault would accept the position, but he would have to be in complete charge of the menu and the kitchen. Mademoiselle Louise was indispensable to him in a foreign environment and would therefore have to be found employment in Huron at not less than a certain salary. A suitably furnished two-bedroom house or apartment, which they would share, would have to be available upon their return. All costs occasioned by the interview and resettlement in Huron would be paid by the generous proprietors of *La Garonne*, including an additional amount to reimburse his present employer for leaving prior to the conclusion of his contract. *D'accord.*

The triumph of the committee was communicated to the others at our next meeting. However, those who had not been present at the interview were not wholly persuaded that Monsieur Renault was the right person for the job. In fact, when the volatile Eric heard Monsieur Renault's bill of particulars, he termed him "a rapacious little bastard," and Dwight, who was usually so trusting, voiced the unthinkable proposition that the diplomas didn't exist. This suspicion gained considerable support, and finally, over the committee's indignant protests, Hughes got a majority to approve engaging a private detective in Quebec to look into the matter of Monsieur Renault's credentials and experience.

We had a report back within a week, but the information it contained did not resolve the problem. Monsieur Renault's present employer was quite pleased with him and anticipated a lengthy relationship. His previous employer wouldn't trust him to boil water. The private eye had also interviewed Monsieur Renault personally, under the pretext of checking his application for a work permit on behalf of the U. S. Department of Labor. In that interview, he had brought up the matter of diplomas without success. In fact, when he mentioned these documents, Monsieur Renault had shown him the door. The private detective, to compensate for his failure to blacken utterly the chef's professional standing, gratuitously added that his investigation had also revealed that Mademoiselle Louise was divorced, that she had worked in a number of third class, or worse, Quebec restaurants, and that she seemed to be quite at home in Monsieur Renault's apartment.

With no other chefs in sight and faced with an absolute need to reduce our indebtedness by opening as soon as possible, we decided to compromise. Monsieur Renault and his companion would be welcomed and their requests fulfilled, but we would test his talent by having him put on four luncheons and four dinners for ourselves and our wives. Our motive would remain hidden, since we would simply say that we wanted to give him an opportunity to acquaint himself with the kitchen and the restaurant's facilities before the place opened to the public.

Three of our wives undertook to find an accommodation

for the chef and Mademoiselle Louise. In order to avoid any involved explanations, we simply told them to find a nice place for the chef and his wife. They located a new apartment in a pleasant area of Huron and busily undertook to furnish it in a manner which they hoped would please the couple. As they hung drapes, washed windows, and waxed floors, they chatted merrily about Mrs. Renault, what a brave little woman she was to leave Quebec, and how they might help her from feeling too lonely in the strange town. Of course, they would all take French lessons from her, and then they could also introduce her to the Friends of France Society. Having cleaned, decorated, and furnished the apartment, they even provided a few bars of perfumed soap for the bathroom, because they knew Madam Renault would appreciate the gesture.

The matter of the trial meals was put to Monsieur Renault immediately upon his return. Ricardo presented the request in French, providing an elegant rigamarole which would have done credit to an ambassador for obfuscation and circumlocution. Monsieur Renault heard him out with apparent ingenuousness. In his response, he agreed completely with the idea that it was imperative for him to become familiar with the kitchen before the public opening and that it would be an honor for him to prepare his first meals at *La Garonne* for the discriminating palates of the owners and their wives. However, he added, such matters were not to be taken lightly, and if he were to perform at his best he would need the aid of Mademoiselle Louise to serve our tables. In compensation for her efforts, he was certain we would want to offer her a position as full-time hostess at *La Garonne* at $150 a week, with the privilege of handling table service in the cocktail lounge when she desired. With his hand on his suitcase, what could we say?

8

Monsieur Renault's revenge for our patent mistrust of his culinary skills was extensive and many-faceted. He immediately embarked on a shopping spree which revealed a capacity for spending other people's money rivaling that of Dicky and Micky. Every conceivable kind of kitchen accessory was suddenly essential, including a bandsaw, a ten-gallon mixer with all available special attachments, pots and pans of every shape and size, and mountains of spoons, forks, skimmers, whisks, graters, squeezers, skewers, cleavers, and knives of every dimension and configuration. Trucks waited around the block to take their turn at the kitchen door, and the stairs to the storeroom almost collapsed under the traffic of purveyors' agents bearing cases of exotic items such as canned kumquats, mandarin orange sections, and chestnut *puré*. The shelves in the basement were packed to the ceiling with canned delicacies such as *quenelles de veau*, there was an ocean of turtle soup, and enough dried laurel leaves to stuff a mattress.

Meanwhile, Monsieur Renault lurked about the kitchen in ambush for the owners, to whom he complained, either directly in French or in English through Mademoiselle Louise, about the location, size, facilities, and cost of his apartment. Nor was he pleased with the furnishings and drapes so carefully selected. Dicky was submerged by an avalanche of special requests, which, it was darkly hinted, if not satisfied would precipitate Monsieur le chef's immediate departure.

While all of this transpired, a grim parody was being perpetrated by the prospective waiters. They too had to be flown from Canada at our expense, they too had to be provided suitable accommodation, they too were unable to handle the immigration permits necessary for their employment, a joyless task that fell upon Jack's legal shoulders. Invariably they arrived penniless, and in some cases apparently even without clothes and barefoot. None would consider providing his own tuxedo or black shoes, so these were purchased at our expense at the best haberdasheries. Some of these loyal retainers departed for points unknown even before we opened, taking with them their new wardrobes and advances against wages and leaving us to face the ire of their unpaid landlords.

The trial meals were Monsieur Renault's most telling revenge. We began with a luncheon, served by Mademoiselle Louise and Dicky in the main dining room, which was still in the hectic stages of final renovation. The scene was incongruous. In the center of the room were four tables furnished with brilliant linen clothes and napkins, gleaming china and sparkling silver, ranks of crystal glasses and a host of other dining accessories. Around this oasis crowded a jumble of saw horses, welding tanks, power tools, and banquettes in various stages of completion. The odor of turpentine was overpowering, and the tangle of wires and extension cords which ran under the tables and chairs threatened the diners with instant electrocution. In the adjacent small dining room artisans continued their labors, raising such a din that conversation was all but impossible.

To titillate our palates, Monsieur Renault first provided *aperitifs* and freshly baked cheese and anchovy sticks. Then came *crème soupe Du Barry*, rich beyond belief. This was followed by *tournedos* of beef with individual sauce boats of *sauce bordelaise*, accompanied by a garnish of *pommes frites* and asparagus tips *hollandaise*. Of course, there were rolls and salad to fill in the cracks, and wines to smooth the passages. Dessert consisted of kumquat tarts with vanilla custard and piped whipped cream. We finished our coffee in the late afternoon, barely in time to stagger home for *Tums* and to change for dinner — a repast that was more elaborate and filling than the earlier gorge, and it concluded around midnight. The next noon, we all gamely reappeared, and that night as well, but by the third day there were dropouts, who brazenly claimed previous engagements. A few of us were determined to persevere despite palpitations and incipient gout. We had *veal Cordon Bleu* and *duck à l'orange* and beef Wellington, and every meal opened with a suffocatingly heavy cream soup. The desserts were inevitably beautiful to behold, and, in our overstuffed condition, possibly fatal to consume, but consume them we did, our every mouthful counted by the beady-eyed Renault, who hovered on the periphery to serve with his own hands enormous portions of the *pièce de résistance* and to cajole us into second helpings of every course.

Having learned the dire penalties attendant upon provoking Monsieur Renault, we were helpless putty in his hands. Through the magic of the long distance telephone, he summoned fellow conspirators to his staff, all accomplished as *sauciers, sous-chefs,* or *garde mangés*. None of these even pretended to a knowledge of English, and all required, according to information relayed by

Mademoiselle Louise, outfits, apartments, working papers, and advances. In our desperation to ensure enough personnel to open, we acceded to their extortionate demands and even resorted to outright bribes. Meanwhile, the storerooms and reefers were filled to overflowing with items essential for the preparation of *la haute cuisine*. The Palermo Laundry Service from Metropolis had provided a Mont Blanc of dazzlingly white linen, the sound system which rendered subdued dinner music was ready to give forth its aural delicacies, and the liquor license had formally completed the final stage of its transfer to our ownership. *La Garonne* was ready for its public debut.

9

Although we were reconciled to the fact that our debut would have to be something less than a Hollywood premiere, an unobtrusive opening was hardly to be considered in view of the sums invested and the luxury of the establishment. Moreover, we all felt that the extent of our individual financial contributions and long-term obligations justified at least a little basking in the praise which would accompany a formal affair. Since so many of Huron's citizens had apparently been fasting in anticipation of *La Garonne's* fare, we decided to avoid a stampede by starting with a week of invitational preview dinners.

Lists of friends, acquaintances, and notables were composed, and the efforts to divide them into compatible groups of not more than one hundred made the tasks of a chief of protocol seem child's play. Invitations were prepared, but they had to be discarded when it was discovered they did not follow socially approved wording. A second printing was hastily ordered and dispatched at the eleventh hour after frantic efforts. A few ghastly oversights were made, such as forgetting an invitation to the mayor or bringing together the local Montagues and Capulets on the same evening. But these gaffes came to light only later.

For reasons of his own, Monsieur Renault was adamant that the menu for each of the six evenings be different, which increased the costs and confused the staff, none of whom was in any sense at home in the unfamiliar surroundings. We felt that $15 a couple was a legitimate charge if an *aperitif* and wine were included, and we inferred to Monsieur Renault that we would appreciate his cooperation in keeping expenses controlled proportionately. But he was determined to establish an instant reputation, even at the price of immediate bankruptcy. Dicky, as well, only gave lip service to pleas for economy, for the preview week was also to provide him the opportunity to star as *maître d' hotel* and manager, and nothing was too good for his audience.

The first dinners went relatively smoothly and were well received, and on those we broke even, not counting salaries and overhead. But on Wednesday, when The Friends of France Society took over the whole restaurant, we plunged into the red. That night Monsieur Renault outdid himself, adding a game course, extra wines (not *ordinaires*) and liqueurs. On Thursday and Friday, the losses continued as our gallant chef built up to the finale on Saturday, a black tie affair at $30 a couple.

The ultimate evening began auspiciously enough at seven with a parade of cars down the main thoroughfare of Huron to the doors of *La Garonne*. Attendants were on hand to assist the begowned ladies to the carpeted sidewalk, and others took the cars away as the gentlemen escorted their ladies to the canopied entrance. By half past seven, the car parkers were unable to keep up with the arrivals, many of whom simply took a parking check from the man in charge and left their vehicles in the street. At eight, there were three police cruisers on the block, not directing traffic but issuing summons for illegal parking and keys in the ignition. They were kind enough not to impound the vehicles. As host, *La Garonne* naturally felt obligated to take care of the tickets, and even with Jack handling the matter (with friends in court) the fines cost us several hundred unbudgeted dollars.

While the police were doing their duty on the street, inside the restaurant a congenial chaos reigned. To begin with, the invited number exceeded our seating capacity, a problem which we had hoped might be resolved, as it had on previous evenings, by sudden illness, the defection of baby-sitters, or domestic discord. But on Saturday night, everyone came, including some invited for Tuesday or Thursday but who had been unable to attend. There were even several couples whom nobody recognized.

Despite the pack, the atmosphere was charged with conviviality and anticipation, and the tension was heightened when a beaming Monsieur Renault passed through the throng bearing an elaborately decorated tray of lobster in aspic topped by a tower of *fruits de mer*. Waiters hustled about dispensing *apéritifs*, and the mob around the bar, where cocktails were complimentary, was impenetrable. Mademoiselle Louise, dressed in the traditional costume of Normandy maidens, served at the tiny tables in the cocktail lounge and dispensed ethnic greetings to *messieurs* and *mesdames*.

At a quarter to nine, the multitude had been seated and there wasn't a vacant chair in either dining room. On the principle of "family holds back," Jack and I had surrendered our table to accommodate some of the unexpected guests, and so we were left standing. For me it was bad enough to be stood up at my own debut, but it was especially disconcerting to Jack, who had invited his brother-in-law and wife to sit with us at our table. The problem was compounded by the circumstance that, over the years, Jack and his brother-in-law had been engaged in a game of one-upmanship, points being won by involvement in successful or exotic business ventures. No permanent winner had ever emerged, and each new achievement was met by the other's facetious criticism, ego-deflating cavils, and snide innuendos. Jack had been looking forward to the grand opening of *his* restaurant as at least a tactical victory in this contest, and he expected, if not overt praise for the grandeur of the establishment, at least tacit approval of its elegance. But from the moment he had set foot in the door, the obdurate relative had refused to vouchsafe even a grudging compliment.

Jack's eager, but thoughtless, question about the decor had elicited an off-handed, "A little loud, maybe?" to which was added, "Did you bring Sally here from Sausalito to decorate the place or did she just send pictures?" Now, unseated with the rest of us, he indulged his cruel humor to the hilt. "Jack, did they take our table away because you didn't have a reservation?" "Are you sure you were invited?" and "Maybe we'd better go somewhere else where I know the owner."

Mademoiselle Louise came to our rescue and thoughtfully improvised a place for six in the cocktail lounge, which was now abandoned. It was not too uncomfortable, and it was a lot quieter than the dining rooms, so we were not unhappy — and, more importantly, our wives were not unhappy either.

The lobster, accompanied by *pâté* sticks, was served to exclamations of wonder and tasted with reverence — at least that was what happened in the part of the dining room I could see from the lounge. Our own servings were more pleasing to the eye than the palate, and the word "elastic" comes to mind. The next treat was Monsieur Renault's beloved *crème Du Barry*, as overpoweringly rich as ever. The soup dishes were removed and a hush fell over the diners. What followed was certainly a first for Huron, a triumphal procession of white garmeted attendants shouldering roast pigs on garnished trays — not suckling pigs but shoats, whose weight caused the bearers to stagger, threatening to crush the diners along the route of this safari. It was a real-life revival of a 1939 Metro-Goldwyn-Mayer spectacular on the orgies of the Roman Empire.

Jack and I had learned of Monsieur Renault's proposal to serve suckling pig, and we had vetoed it, as if that made any difference. Word of our negativism had reached the chef, and now our isolation in the bar, of which he was aware, made it possible for him to punish us by an alimentary *manoeuvre*. The guests in the dining rooms were served generous and apparently tasty portions of the pigs, but we got large disks of gristle and bone cut with the bandsaw from just behind the ears of the sacrificial beasts.

Jack was crushed, and his delighted brother-in-law mercilessly rubbed it in.

"Do you get this cut of pork by special order?" "Meat always tastes better closer to the bone, don't you think?" "Don't bother about seconds, a little goes a long way." "I'd take mine home in a doggy bag, except that we don't have a jackal."

Dessert was the kumquat tart, sufficiently attractive and certainly exotic enough to prevent negative comment from novice gourmets. The repast concluded with coffee and liqueurs. Throughout the meal and afterward, public compliments were lavish, especially for the neo-bordello decor. The aspic and pig were also a success, and Monsieur Renault was in seventh heaven, presiding over informal receptions in the kitchen for those guests who pilgrimaged there to deliver expressions of admiration. When he set foot in the dining rooms, he received smatterings of applause. For him, it was a climactic moment.

Apart from the chef's gristly revenge, Jack and I had a good evening, but our fun was somewhat tempered by our concern as owners that everything should go smoothly and everyone be completely satisfied. His brother-in-law had no such anxieties, and in fact, his pleasure increased at any evidence of imperfect service or operational confusion. Jack bore up rather well under his constant digs, recharging his pierced ego with the many warming compliments of the other guests. I was amused to learn, however, that the brother-in-law was the only person who had to pay his own fine for parking illegally and leaving his keys in the ignition.

Opening Night

La Seine:
haute cuisine in Ann Arbor, Michigan

It was *ALL* her fault!

Crystal stemware—only
the best for La Seine.

In a swanky joint like this, you wear a tuxedo.

51

I hope they saved a table for us.

A couple of investors, happy as clams. *Little did we know!*

Fortunate non-investors.

In culinary terms, 'my fat was in the fire.'

Find the investor in this group.
Ivan called him Dwight.

The best ever since prohibition.

Who's going to wash all these glasses?

Where is that pig? Are we ever going to get served?

That pig made the
supreme sacrifice
**The investors were
soon to follow.**

Genuine French waitresses -
imported directly from
Quebec City at some cost!

10

The preview dinners were like a wedding reception at which the bride and groom are already having second thoughts. In the weeks which followed, we pretended to be honey-mooning in Acapulco, but we were really jetting towards Reno.

The owners had a variety of opinions regarding the week-that-was, and these ranged from "fabulous" to "fiasco," depending upon what part of the pig we had been served. There was complete agreement, however, that we had lost a healthy sum of money on our opening, although some $5,000 had been paid in by the week's preview guests. The bookkeeper suggested that we enter the deficit under "Account 999, Promotion of Business," which made everything tidy and comforting.

For the next few weeks, we had customers waiting in line, curious to see in person the notorious decor and experience cuisine *classique française*. Then, too, the forthcoming holidays generated a considerable post-cocktail party trade, and we ourselves were patronizing the place heavily, showing off our new toy to out of town friends and professional associates. Despite the near capacity volume of business, we continued to lose money, a situation we were determined to rectify at once, even though experienced restaurateurs like Dicky insisted that every new establishment ran in the red for the first few months.

Monsieur Renault's department was the first object of our

scrutiny. The cost-conscious Hughes volunteered to make a clandestine analysis of the overflowing garbage cans clustered around the back door, and this confirmed his suspicions that enormous waste of expensive raw materials and prepared foods was occurring. Hughes felt that his contribution ended with the discovery of the offense and refused to confront Monsieur Renault himself. Besides, he correctly believed it was up to Dicky to exercise his managerial responsibility and remonstrate with the chef. The other owners, having some inkling of Monsieur Renault's whimsical temperament, thought Dicky needed moral support, and so I was detailed to accompany him. This was certainly a far cry from my earlier Mitty-like dreams of *camaraderie* between the gourmet (myself) and the chef, the friendly consultations about menus, and that sort of bosh. Now instead of approving his sauces, I was asked to criticize his garbage.

The confrontation began as a dialogue, Mademoiselle Louise interpreting. Dicky led into the subject tactfully, qualifying his remarks with expressions of esteem for the chef's talents, for the concern he had always manifested with respect to the establishment's reputation, and for the owners' sincere satisfaction with his services. But Monsieur Renault shortly suspicioned a worm in the apple, and as the critical essence of Dicky's persiflage became increasingly evident, he commenced to purple and chew his lips. When the brutal word *gaspiller*, "to waste", assaulted his ears, he had heard enough, and a torrent of recriminations burst forth. How dare anyone interfere in the way he ran his kitchen? The owners knew nothing about costs. What is worse, they had insulted his honor. Did they think he did not know they had sent a private detective to Quebec to investigate him? Did they think he didn't understand the reason he had to serve those meals just to themselves and their wives? Did they think he did not know they were plotting behind his back? Did they think he was going to let his honor be stained and do nothing about it? As he fed on his ire, he advanced on Dicky, his fluttering hands making spastic gropings toward his arsenal of knives and cleavers. The thought of being reduced to steak tartar was too much for Dicky, who abruptly fled in mortal terror. I was five jumps ahead of him.

Monsieur Renault was resolved to maintain the offensive, and having disposed of Dicky, he besieged Hughes. When our financial watchdog was luckless enough to encounter him in the kitchen, scandalous scenes took place. It became Monsieur Renault's habit to indulge his bad humor by snatching the chef's hat from his head and flinging it onto the floor, a gesture which was accompanied by a *Provençal* jig and imprecations from the docks of Marseilles. The tall white hat, soiled by contact with the greasy tiles, was necessarily replaced by a fresh one, and the spiraling laundry bills were a reliable index of the chef's increasing dissatisfaction.

When the novelty of this antic ceased to affect Hughes' equanimity, the chef chose every occasion to announce that he was quitting, a fairly safe gesture, since Hughes pretended he didn't understand and the chef pretended to believe him.

His *haute cuisine* began to rely more and more upon the stock-pile of canned goods in the basement, and the consistency with which a certain share of dinners were sent burned to the dining rooms suggested either a deliberate plan or the total absence of concern for *La Garonne's* reputation. The number of patrons, which had already diminished with the passing of the holidays, was reduced to a trickle. The owners commissioned Ricardo to establish direct, man-to-man communication with Monsieur Renault, thus eliminating Mademoiselle Louise from the discussion, and to make known to the chef that we could not continue to lose money indefinitely.

Ricardo, confident of his powers of persuasion and personal charm, opened the conversation by venturing to suggest we might attract more business by catering to a broader clientele.

"Would *Monsieur le chef* be kind enough to include a moderately priced *table d' hôte* dinner on his menu?"

"Non! Le menu c'est à la carte sans exceptions."

"Would Monsieur reconsider the pricing of some items, perhaps lowering his *soupe a l'onion au trois étoiles* to one dollar?"

"Non, les prix sont mon affair."

"But *Monsieur,* although your *soupe à l'onion au trois étoiles* is a masterpiece and veritably a meal in itself, it is still a bowl of soup, and people won't pay $2.25 for a bowl of soup, even if it is called *soupe au trois étoiles."*

"Absolutement non! Je sais mon metier, merde alors!"

We explored other possibilities. The menus, which were the size of travel posters and whose colors rivaled those of an over-sexed peacock, were being printed separately for each night, with the date and day of the week conveniently provided at the top for those diners in need of that information. It seemed logical to adopt a fixed menu, thus cutting printing expenses and possibly, although this seemed less certain, reducing food costs by eliminating loss through wasted perishables. Monsieur Renault would have none of it. Nothing would change.

His was a difficult personality.

11

Nothing fails like failure, and failure does not bring out the best in human nature. Our continuing losses made our Wednesday meetings in Jack's office acquire an acrimonious and inquisitorial character. There were several consistent candidates for the role of Grand Inquisitor, while those who were officers of the corporation were often cast in the role of heretics. But most frequently it was Dicky who was threatened with the dread *auto da fé*.

In retaliation, Dicky complained that some of the owners were interfering in managerial matters, encouraging complaints of dissident employees, and generally undermining his attempts to maintain discipline. In truth, the chandeliered halls of *La Garonne* had become a Borgia's court of intrigue and espionage, with cooks, waiters, busboys, bartenders, potwashers, and even parking attendants seeking protectors among the owners, informing on one another, and concocting lurid tales of thievery, doubtless based on personal experience. But Dicky's charges, however justified, simply stimulated counter charges and a flood of complaints about his ineptitude and deficiencies as manager. His antagonists insisted that our losses were quite evidently his doing, a result of his chronic inattention to detail and lack of sound business practice, a perfect example of which was his rather frequent departure from the restaurant before closing time.

The *quiche lorraine* episode, as it came to be called, was

one example of the criticism leveled at Dicky which tended to distract our attention from major problems of management and even generated the sympathy which perpetuated his tenure. It was known that food was being pilfered by the employees, which was not surprising, since from the first *La Garonne* had been a domestic Care Package for all takers. The reefers, refrigerators, and storerooms were supposed to be locked every night at closing, and the manager had been charged with seeing that this was done. Sometimes he did, and sometimes he didn't. In order to prove his neglect in the matter, the anti-manager faction, led by Hughes and Ricardo, conducted an inventory check. Following this, they called for a special meeting, hinting that incontrovertible proof of Dicky's incompetence would be disclosed, the nature of which indeed suggested his collusion with sinister (but unspecified) factions bent on our destruction.

An atmosphere of strained curiosity prevailed as we assembled for the extraordinary Monday meeting. Hughes and Ricardo looked as if they had just eaten the canary and were obviously anxious to begin. Ralph, who invariably took Dicky's side, had left his usual grin at home, and Willis, too, was conspicuously unlaughing. They clustered in a corner with Dicky, who had a somewhat hangdog expression, and conferred earnestly until the meeting was called to order by Dwight, the current president. Formalities were bypassed and we proceeded immediately to "New Business." Hughes then rose gravely from his chair and, with funereal mien, moved to a position where he faced the rest of us.

"Gentlemen. As you recall, at the time we formed this corporation, you were gracious enough to trust me with handling financial matters. You are also aware that since the inception of this project I have continually pointed out the constant failure of the manager to hold expenses within reason or to consult with me regarding expenditures. Against my strongest admonitions, you have chosen to take his side on many occasions and to ignore the fiscal implications."

Hughes' solemn expression lightened somewhat as he turned to face Dicky. "Dicky knows that I have the highest regard for him as a person, and I sincerely appreciate his invariable friendliness and politeness to me." The solemn look returned, accompanied by a frown. "But I must say in all candour that he is a failure as a manager and, furthermore, totally irresponsible." He paused, anticipating some reaction to his harsh words.

The respondant was the modish Ralph, whose blazing eyes were clearly evident despite the heavy tint of his glasses.

"How the devil could he manage anything with you constantly interfering? You've undercut him from the beginning. We've got to give the poor kid a chance to show what he can do. And the best thing you could do would be to get off his back."

Hughes favored Ralph with a pained smile. "Dicky has had that chance. In recent weeks, I have purposely refrained from commenting unnecessarily about the way he has been doing things — or, rather, not doing things — and with what result? First, on the matter about which I have remonstrated with him on several occasions, the proper polishing of his shoes before appearing in the dining rooms, I have observed no change. But more significant is the matter I wish to bring up now, the fact that Dicky's failure to lock the coolers at night has encouraged extensive and costly pilferage. The night before last he again left them unlocked.

I checked their contents at that time and again first thing in the morning." Hughes assumed an expression of triumphant revelation. "Three pieces of *quiche lorraine* were missing." He paused for the impact of this to be absorbed. "What is more, gentlemen, several *éclairs* and a dish of *chocolate mousse* were also gone."

A murmur arose among those assembled. Ralph again snatched up the gauntlet. "First of all," he addressed Hughes, "you were chosen to oversee the operation because you were the only person here who wasn't occupied full time with other business. Second, instead of helping you have sat there in the restaurant bugging Dicky about trivia like polished shoes. Now you're making a federal case out of a piece of cheese pie and some stale desserts. And where, for that matter, are the financial reports that you are supposed to provide? I haven't seen one of those in over a month."

Hughes met these words with an indulgent look. "I quite understand the implications of your gracious remark about my being the only owner with sufficient free time to oversee the restaurant. As for the matter of financial reports, we presumably are paying an accountant to provide these. And I might add that this accountant, who was your choice, not mine, has still not delivered the February report, which is now over six weeks late. The issue here, gentlemen, is not my qualification but the irresponsible negligence of Dicky as manager."

A babble persisted until the doctor restored a semblance of order by pounding on the desk. Hughes was allowed to continue, this time detailing what he called abuses of "Account 999, Promotion of Business". His summary did reveal an astounding number of complimentary dinners, free drinks, and gifts of wine.

When he concluded, Dicky, at Ralph's insistence and with Willis's encouragement, took the floor in his own defense. The free dinners, he asserted, were almost entirely given to persons who had labored long and for no compensation during the period of renovation. The only exceptions were three dinners, two of which were given to fellow restaurateurs, a gesture traditional in the business. The third complimentary dinner had been signed for by Hughes, for reasons which Hughes had not chosen to tell him. As for the free drinks and wines, how else was he to calm the customers whose food had been burned or who complained about bad service? In short, every dinner could be justified, every gift of drink and bottle rationalized.

The moment Dicky finished his defense, Jack seized control of the meeting by the simple expedient of raising his voice until he was given the floor. When everyone became silent, he thanked Dicky for his report and suggested that he had pressing obligations at the restaurant, so he could be excused. The hint was taken and Dicky departed. As he closed the door, Jack turned testily to Hughes and Ricardo.

"You called this meeting and got us all down here to listen to this kind of petty nonsense — missing *éclairs*. It's worse than the strawberries in *The Caine Mutiny*. I completely agree that it's Dicky's responsibility to lock up at night, every night, but we don't have to have a special meeting to convey that message. Sure, Dicky has to shape up right now or get lost. However, it is true that some of you seem to have been making a special effort to undermine his authority. Ricardo, we know about those parties for some of the waiters at your house. Now, let's give Dicky one final chance to prove himself. I propose that for the next month we follow the principle that Hughes stays out of the picture as much as possible and takes no action, especially with the employees, unless he works through Dicky. Ricardo is to stay out of the business, period. He is not to talk to the help, either on the job or elsewhere." Jack turned to Dwight, "That's in the form of a motion."

There wasn't much debate. Hughes and Ricardo nursed their bruised feelings in silence, and, under the circumstances, Ralph and Willis could not have hoped for a better deal for their protégé. Eric was perplexed and irritated, voicing his objection to the motion as he moved his massive frame with ominous frustration around Jack's office.

"Jesus G. Christ, we've already waited too long. Do you need a better example than the fact that we as owners have to tell Dicky as manager that he is supposed to lock up at night? What in hell are we paying a manager for? I don't care if Ricardo has a hundred parties for the waiters. That's no reason to keep Dicky. I say he goes and we use his thousand a month salary to get someone who doesn't have to be told to use his keys, for Christ's sake."

Jack asked a pointed question. "All right Eric, we dump Dicky today, but are you prepared to go down to *La Garonne* right now and take over the management? Or do you have someone in mind who can take over today? If not, it doesn't make any difference how right you are, because until we can get someone else, Dicky is better than no one at all."

Eric retreated to his chair, shaking his head. We voted, Hughes and Ricardo opposing, Eric abstaining, and the motion carrying handily with Ralph's and Willis's votes supporting those of Jack, Dwight, and myself. The spirit of compromise had prevailed again.

12

The jolly confrontations between the chef and the owners came to an abrupt and unanticipated end. Someone confided to the immigration authorities that Monsieur Renault was not living entirely alone, as behooved a bachelor guest in this virtuous country, and he was told to hustle himself beyond the continental limits. The parting was hardly sweet sorrow, but it left us chefless.

Dicky's response was admirable and revealed an unsuspected versatility and organizational ingenuity. He took over the kitchen himself, conscripting as his aids a bartender and the bookkeeper. Happily, we still retained the services of the *garde mangé*, Guillaume, a morose young man of pasty exterior who throughout the Renault regime had unobtrusively and methodically pursued his craft in an alcove of the kitchen.

For three weeks this team fought to overcome the challenge imposed by Monsieur Renault's elaborate menus. With flushed faces and burned fingers they scurried about, wielding knives and cleavers with no regard for the risk to their extremities or each other, sacrificing eyebrows and hair as they courageously peered into the pulsating broilers, resolutely advanced into clouds of steam to tend vats of boiling stock. Spattered with grease, stained with sauces, soaked with perspiration, nicked and singed, they carried on, but their efforts were in vain. From the dining rooms arose a chorus of complaints which could not be silenced by propitiatory offerings of even the most expensive wines. Diners clutched at their throats as the monstrous mutations of traditional sauces violated their senses, they screened their eyes with napkins at the sight of the dishes placed before them. Waiters had to guard the doors to the kitchen to prevent bodily harm to the heroic workers within.

Under the circumstances, any change could not help but be for the better. No chefs were available, or perhaps word was out that *La Garonne's* reputation had been indelibly ruined. Personnel agencies could offer no one. At the moment of final despair, a purveyor confided to Dicky that the Hotel Royal, the finest hostelry in nearby Metropolis, had a disaffected chef who might be available for a price. Dicky relayed the information to Hughes, who dismissed the possibility on the grounds that *La Garonne* was sufficiently insolvent without having to pay for a chef with a national reputation.

So Dicky went to Jack, who instantly cancelled all appointments and sent Dicky after the purveyor to arrange an immediate interview, that afternoon if possible. Meanwhile, Jack called me to share the good news and to sample the reaction of the directors to our "buying the high priced spread," as he put it. I was all in favor, since the alternatives were either to get a chef or close, but my enthusiasm was qualified somewhat by apprehensions about the cost of a five-star performer. Jack swept aside my reservations by citing his thumbnail fiscal philosophy: you have to spend money to make money, and the higher the price the better the quality.

With the support of the directors, as evidenced by the findings of his one-man poll, Jack saw no reason for further delay. The purveyor-informant had been located and had briefed Dicky on the layout of the Hotel Royal. Word had been passed to the chef that a committee from *La Garonne* was on the way. Operation Underbelly was "Go!"

Jack and Dicky were aware that their deed must be accomplished with all the subtlety of a reconnaissance mission to a hostile beach, for were the Royal's manager to catch them in the act of inviting his chef's defection, they would be publicly exposed on the spot and the name of *La Garonne* anathematized throughout the restaurant industry. Thus, when they reached the hotel, their approach was to the rear of the edifice, and there they entered a door which opened on stairs leading into the bowels of the building. Their path was then subterranean, along endless corridors, around many turns, past whole communities of chattering machines and frantic compressors. At last their noses confirmed that they were beneath the objective, and stealthily they ascended the nearest stairs. The door onto the landing opened easily and silently, and through it they could see a brilliantly lighted kitchen. The most dangerous part of their mission had been accomplished.

Among the many white-garmeted and tall-hatted persons in the room, they had no difficulty in distinguishing the chef of chefs, André François Dupuis. Shorter than the others, but with the tallest hat, he stood before a spanking new electric stove holding a massive frying pan and observing its contents with bitter disdain. He glanced at the interlopers, assumed who they were, and addressed himself to no one in particular.

"Eez amposseebl to kook ear. Damn stof take forevair. I kan't feed five dining room from zeez ole. Zair eez no room to work. Kom, we talk."

He led them along a passage behind the kitchen to a room on whose door was "Executive Chef". On being ushered in, they were confronted by a wall covered with diplomas, certificates, gastronomic awards, pictures of celebrities endorsed with intimate personal messages, telegrams of congratulation, and colored pictures of the chef standing before bountiful buffets of culinary masterpieces. They were properly impressed.

André François Dupuis told them his history. He had begun his apprenticeship in France at the age of seven and had received his first white hat at fourteen. The hat had grown taller as he had continued his career at the best hotels of the world, but it was in the United States, with the patronage of Luis Diat of the Ritz, that he had become *chef de cuisine*, the ultimate rank in his profession. He had recently left a comfortable administrative position with an Eastern hotel chain, because he enjoyed exercising his art, and in the East the union had forbidden him, as executive chef, to touch so much as a spoon. At the Hotel Royal he had been thoroughly frustrated by the cramped efficiency kitchen and electric stoves. He was ready to consider an offer and would inspect *La Garonne* on Sunday.

Jack and I were on hand to greet him. The shambles of Saturday night had remained untouched by the porter, and the waiters had departed without clearing the tables. Random utensils lay about on the carpet in the company of soiled napkins and an occasional glass. Bits of rolls and crumbs were everywhere, and half consumed desserts sulked amid the litter on the rumpled tablecloths. Empty bottles reclined in wicker holders or stood neck down in tableside coolers.

While waiting for the chef to arrive, Jack and I had occupied ourselves by attempting to sort through a heap of invoices and bills, our purpose being to discover how to make a $30,000 extension of our line of credit defray $45,000 in accounts payable. When he appeared, we discreetly flung a wine-stained cloth over the evidence of insolvency and invited him to sit down. His codfish eyes slowly surveyed the condition of the dining room.

"Waiters are like whores," he said flatly. "Zey know you're in trobl, zey treat you like zeez. Onlee monee matter to zem." We silently commended his observation.

Despite the blitzed appearance of the dining rooms and bar, some of the dearly purchased elegance was still apparent, and this obviously created a good impression. The tour of the kitchen was another matter. It looked as if frenzied animals had been baited there, and by comparison the dining rooms seemed antiseptically clean and orderly. André François Dupuis shuffled aside broken crockery and bones in his progress toward the stoves, pausing with incredulity before a vat of *coq au vin* that would have wiped the smile from a hyena.

"Eet steenks bad," he asserted solemnly. "Zeez plaze need steam kleening."

His inspection of the stoves and ovens was brief and professional. "Zair old, but one kan kook on zem." We breathed easier. He pulled open the door of the walk-in cooler and recoiled: "Zrow evairyzeeng out!" In the basement, his tour through the storeroom was accompanied by a sorrowful and mute shaking of the head, and his only comment on noticing the tower of canned kumquats, the legacy of Monsieur Renault, was a perplexed, "What for zeez stuf?"

For three hours, Jack and I alternated monologues, trying to convey some idea of our original hopes, and gradually the chef became animated in a phlegmatic sort of way. When he himself began proposing how the image could be restored and improved, we knew we had him (or was it the other way around?). His price was high, $400 a week, but he wouldn't consider a reduction of his present income. He would give notice at the Hotel Royal and be at *La Garonne* in three weeks.

13

Word that *La Garonne* was about to acquire the services of a famous chef spread instantly among the staff, and already the day after our interview, morale at the restaurant was markedly improved, especially among the waiters. Dicky had his own reasons for jubilation, foreseeing an imminent end to his efforts as galley slave and anticipating the regrowth of eyebrows lost while cremating a chicken in the broiler. The owners also soon learned that Dupuis had responded positively following his inspection of the premises, and the general reaction was "Thank God!" Therefore, when we met on Wednesday morning to ratify officially the abduction of André François Dupuis, we convened in an atmosphere of rekindled hope.

There was, however, one grave visage present, and, typically, it belonged to Hughes. In glum silence, he listened as Jack animatedly related details of our interview with Dupuis and expounded the virtues and qualifications of our choice. When Jack finished, Hughes moved in like a leaden cloud darkening a spring morn.

"Gentlemen, I am frankly dismayed that Jack and Ivan took it upon themselves to encourage this Dupuis to think he would be employed at *La Garonne*. Even if I were positive that everything Jack has just said were true and objective, in good conscience I could still not support hiring him. With the debts we have accumulated, we cannot afford anyone at $400 a week. I must now confess, gentlemen, that I had known about Dupuis long before Dicky told me about him, and then, as now, I categorically rejected him as too expensive and of dubious ability. Has any of you eaten at the Hotel Royal? Can any of you say it has a reputation for its food?"

We remained mute. Hughes continued, his tone increasingly pedantic as we failed to respond to his argument. "I must say in all candour that the whole idea is the height of fiscal irresponsibility. It is typical," and here he directed a sour look at Jack, "of the reckless extravagance and carelessness which has prevailed from the start. I have been thwarted in every effort to impose economies. From this I conclude that you as a group wish for some reason to squander your money. I do not and will not. Furthermore, my relationship with Dicky has become intolerable. In the past month, he hasn't once asked my prior approval for any expenditure, except for one snide gesture when he asked me to approve buying a twenty cent notebook. His shoes are now deliberately unshined. I will not be mocked in this manner by someone half my age."

Visibly agitated by his own rhetoric, Hughes mournfully contemplated the carpet and took several deep breaths. He then nodded affirmatively and withdrew a long envelope from an inner pocket of his suit.

"Gentlemen, this is my resignation. Whether you accept it or not is up to you, but I have confidence in your good judgement and our past friendly relations. My conditions are as follows. I will agree to hiring this expensive chef, but in return you must agree to economize by dismissing Dicky as manager. If you prefer Dicky to me, then you may pick up my letter. Naturally, I expect that if you accept my resignation, knowing that it was forced upon me, you will do the proper thing by releasing me from any obligations for our line of credit or for any debts, past, present, or future." Hughes then placed the envelope on Jack's desk and left the room.

While Ralph had watched this performance, his initial Cheshire grin had metamorphosed into a derisive sneer. Hughes had hardly shut the door when he leaped to his feet and, grinning hugely, declared, "What's to choose? Pick up the letter! Of all the dishonest crap I've ever heard, this takes the cake. Not one word, mind you, not a single word about Dicky keeping the kitchen going after Renault left, not a single word about that. But what does he talk about? The same old unshined shoes. And you know why Dicky hasn't gone to him for approval of purchases? Because every time he does Hughes gives him an hour lecture on economy and starts bugging him about trivia. Dicky simply hasn't the time for that crap, especially trying to run the kitchen as well. So let's pick up the letter."

Eric wanted more information before taking action. "Ricardo, you've been close to Hughes lately. Is this an act or does he mean it? Because if he means it, let's dump Dicky. As I see it, we have no alternative but to get this chef. Face it, we're up the creek so far it's only a trickle. And the whole goddamm bottom's gone out of the canoe."

Willis didn't wait for Ricardo's response. "Oh, Hughes is just acting like an old woman, as usual. You can't believe the kind of pressure he's been putting on Dicky. My own feeling is that Hughes wants to manage the restaurant himself. I say accept his resignation and good riddance."

Jack then queried Ricardo briefly as to the seriousness of Hughes' intentions, and Ricardo said he had tried to talk Hughes out of writing the letter, but Hughes was determined. If he didn't get his way, he would quit.

The discussion wandered on for some time, but the more we talked, the more impossible it seemed to find a way to resolve the dilemma posed by Hughes' ultimatum. We were all convinced we had to hire the new chef, but feelings were mixed about sacking Dicky in the bargain. The upshot was that we decided to hire the chef and keep Dicky. As far as Hughes was concerned, it was left to him to stay or withdraw. He withdrew.

The same week, we had excellent news from André François Dupuis. The manager of the Hotel Royal had received notification of the chef's impending departure in a manner so ungracious as to make the customary two weeks' of terminal employment unnecessary. The chef had at once gone to New York in search of staff and had located a cook-butcher and an experienced *saucier* who could join him immediately at *La Garonne*. These, with the continued aid of Guillaume, the *garde mangé*, would provide sufficient staff for the time being.

There was no question that we had acquired a chef who knew what he was about. The kitchen was immediately cleaned to the point that the health inspector stopped flourishing his padlocks, the purveyors were advised to stop giving shoddy merchandise and short weight, the waiters were admonished to start hustling or else, and the cashier was made liable for any unregistered orders leaving the kitchen. André François Dupuis came in like March.

His cuisine was not truly *classique française*. Long years of expatriation, catering to the local tastes of Cairo, Prague, Buenos Aires, and later New York, Chicago, and Hollywood had altered the traditional qualities of his dishes, just as those years had deprived him of a characteristically French accent. But what he prepared had French names, was tasty and attractive, and satisfied anyone who didn't expect *La Pyramide* in *La Garonne*. Some of us, of course, had hoped for at least a modest *Pyramide* in Huron, and what with Dupuis' experience and talent there seemed every reason at least to try to approach the sublime heights of France's best known temple of gastronomic miracles. One day I cautiously queried the chef on the matter, tactfully suggesting that there would be no objection on the owners' part if he wanted to prepare his dishes strictly according to traditional recipes. He got the point and gave me a forthright answer.

"Ivan, zeez zings I know better than you. I kan do the *classique* way, but eez too deeferent for Americans. Zey don't want too much strange taste. Maybe one deeferent dish for each meal, the rest very good but not too new for zem. You know who like my kooking? Chews. Yes, I know ow to feed Chews. Zey kan't resist my krisp duck, partikular when served with sweet potato and bananas *Grand Marnier*. You know, I won prize for zat. Chews know good food and zey will pay. Onlee troubl eez zey don't drink, except wine. But I'll get Chews to kom ear and we'll do planty business. You leaf zat up to me. Ride now we need kustomers more zan sauces."

Word of the restaurant's resurrection soon spread, encouraged by advertising and a satisfied clientele. Reservations even became advisable, at least on weekends, and a group of devoted patrons started to develop. Business received a real boost from an unsolicited, rave review in a widely circulated entertainment guide, and goodly numbers began making the trek from Metropolis. Meanwhile, the graph of gross receipts plotted a line from $4,000 a week to $5,000 and then even past $6,000, tantalizingly ascending towards the presumed break-even point of $8,000. There was guarded optimism among the owners, and we no longer fled conversations if the subject of *La Garonne* were broached. It looked as if we might make it.

14

In the good old days, every church congregation had its nosy-noisy busybody, the publicly pious old hen who found a mission in scratching up the sins of others and then running around cackling about them. The modern counterpart is the Do-Gooder, a self-appointed vigilantee whose mission is to discover and bring to pillory those who would transgress the code of human justice. *La Garonne* was the target of such a guardian of public morals.

One morning the following letter appeared in the restaurant's mail:

Dear Sir:

We are writing in response to the ads you have been running in (the local newspaper), inviting the university community to dine at La Garonne. As members of that community who enjoy and admire French cuisine, we welcomed the presence of a good French restaurant in our town.

However, while we like good food and pleasant atmosphere, we dislike institutions that play upon people's pretensions to aristocracy, especially when they do so at the expense of the dignity and physical comfort of a fellow human being. Many an icy evening we have driven by your establishment, and have seen a human being, dressed in the costume of an antebellum house slave, shivering by the door of La Garonne. The reason for his being there is clearly to pander to the assumed desire of your customers to pretend, if only for an hour or two, that they are rich plantation owners attending a feast at a neighboring mansion, to be served by a corps of uniformed lackeys. The man who must stand outside in the cold in his slave costume is not considered. He is reduced to an object, a prop having no emotions, no dignity, no soul. He is simply an instrument to satisfy the degenerate cravings of some people, who having accumulated enough money to dine in elegance at La Garonne, want to buy with it the illusion of return to an earlier time, when the exploitation of the many by the few could be indulged in more comfortably and openly. Probably there are those who are attracted by such pleasures. As for us, it turns our stomachs and makes us quite unable to eat. Certainly we have no desire to dine at La Garonne. We condemn your disgusting exploitation of a fellow human being, who, needing a job so that he can live, is forced into playing the role of slave, made to stand out in the cold and the rain, and for no reason except to gratify the obscene appetites of your customers, and your own perverted sense of elegance and good living.

We urge you to discontinue your present policy, not to fire your "door men," but rather to give them a decent job at a decent wage, and if your doors are too heavy for your customers to open themselves, to replace them with lighter ones. Until then we continue to urge our friends not to patronize La Garonne.

[Signature of husband and wife]

Such pleasant compliments certainly deserved an answer, so I undertook the composition of a "thank you" note.

*Dear Mr. and Mrs. *******,*

    We were grieved to receive your letter condemning our "disgusting exploitation of a fellow human being. . ." etc., etc. If there were any truth or substance to your allegations, there would be cause for concern, but your charges are based on total and willful ignorance of fact.

    First, the employee to whom you refer is not dressed in the "costume of an ante-bellum house slave." The climate in Huron is quite unsuitable for slave costumes of any sort, even if we favored them, which we decidedly do not. Second, the employee is warmly dressed, or should be, and his boots were purchased specially for dryness and warmth. A heat lamp is also provided in the awning under which he stands. Third, and this you might have determined simply by asking, he is not a doorman but a <u>parking attendant</u> who fulfills the responsible role of parking customers' automobiles. An employee of this sort is essential to any enterprise located down-town which involves a high volume of business from people who arrive in cars. You urge us not to fire this person but to provide "a decent job at a decent wage". Again, if you had bothered to in-quire, you would have found that he receives $1.75 an hour in addition to tips; his normal salary exclusive of tips is around $100 a week. If you had looked more carefully, you would have noticed that white employees have also held this position — so much for the "ante-bellum house slave" theory.

    But more disturbing than your uninformed attack on the restaurant's management and clientele, however, is your arroga-tion of the right to judge another human as "an object, a prop having no emotions, no dignity, no soul." In fact, what you have done is exactly what you have accused us of doing. What right *have you to demean anyone because **you** have decided that his employment is unfitting? The employee who currently holds the position of parking attendant is an honest and hard working person who efficiently carries out a necessary and, at times, difficult task. He has the right to expect that his work be respected. **We** respect him and his job; you do not.*

We categorically do not seek to "pander" to customers who wish to pretend that they are rich "plantation owners." If such customers exist, that is their delusion. If their capabilities for fantasy are strong enough, they may possibly transform a parking attendant into a slave, as you seem to have done. For our part, we have simply wanted to provide a needed service for our customers.

We regret that you have determined to ignore facts and misconstrue our intentions.

> *Sincerely yours,*
> *The Management*

Our correspondents evidently found *La Garonne* an uncongenial pen pal, for they never replied. Meanwhile, the owners had some laughs about our no-longer secret plot to pander to obscene appetites. Jack even publicly confessed to an obscene appetite for *escargots*.

15

By the time André François Dupuis arrived, we had learned that it was like trying to hold minnows in a fist to keep an entire staff of French speaking waiters. We had made the effort, Lord knows. For a while during the early days the traffic of our imports from Quebec and Montreal was so heavy that we considered asking for group fares. Another plan was to fly them in on the twenty-one day excursion rate, since none of them seemed to stay much longer than that anyhow. In the course of four months, we imported an entire Foreign Legion of Pierres, Antoines, Henris, and Etiennes. They had faces attached to their names, but time has dissolved the connection, so that now the roster of *La Garonne's* French contingent reads with all the impersonality of the Paris phone directory. Each came, saw, and conquered, at least to the extent of departing richer by a new tuxedo and pair of pointed black shoes.

Their American replacements were seldom from among the Huronese, apparently originating from a national pool of migrant waiters who played musical chairs among the country's more elegant establishments. They came announced and unannounced, and departed with and without notice. Unlike their Gallic brethren, this domestic product did have tuxedos and shoes of their own. In fact, most were impeccable dressers, with frilled shirt fronts and lace cuffs, oversize links, and carefully tailored trousers which tapered down to glistening patent leather pumps with buckles. When they walked, their backsides twitched, and the swing of their hips was perfectly balanced by counter-movements of the shoulders. They were as temperamental as divas, which suited their soprano voices. At a real or fancied offense, they would mince poutily from the dining room to complain to Dicky, and if he withheld consolation they would rush to sob unconsolably on the back stairs, abandoning their customers to perplexed oblivion.

Word spread that welcome awaited them at *La Garonne*, so they flew thither on fairy wings. Members of the sorority with experience as busboys and barboys also flitted onto the scene, and some limp wristed candidates even applied for jobs in the kitchen — and were sent scurrying by an indignant André François Dupuis.

The most egregious specimen of them all was Nicky, who had progressed from busboy to cashier at the kitchen register. A sometime dancer, Nicky had been around since the inception of *La Garonne*, torn between his loyalty to Dicky's establishment and a career in New York. Unable to indulge his Terpsichorean urge in the confines of the cashier's slot, he developed a compensatory talent — the fine art of lighting cigarettes. His performances were marked by all the discipline of the ballet and theatre combined. The show began with a graceful sweep of the right forearm followed by a sharp inclination of the wrist, permitting the extended fingers to grasp and withdraw the hardpack of filter kings from the breast pocket. Two sharp shakes of the pack would expose the filter, the chin would be lifted sharply, and a slow motion of the arm would deliver the still boxed cigarette to slightly opened lips. With the head unmoved, the box would be withdrawn and returned to the breast pocket, from which a lighter was then taken. The left hand would then rise diagonally until the slightly separated first and second fingers engaged the cigarette and firmly anchored it between them. The head and cigarette were frozen as the flame was applied and a lengthy drag taken. The left hand was then flung dramatically away, bearing the cigarette with it, the chin being twisted upwards and to the right, and the smoke deeply inhaled. The cigarette was returned to neutral position in a slow motion that was accompanied by an audible exhalation of smoke.

Nicky was one of the more stable employees and didn't quit oftener than once or twice a month, but the others were like fruit flies, flitting around brainlessly. Some quit, took other jobs, and returned, and others were dismissed for cause and subsequently rehired, and still others yo-yoed out to other jobs and back with rhythmic frequency. It was hard to keep enough W-2 forms on hand to handle the turnover. Dicky didn't help matters by assigning the best tables to his particular favorites or by steering the generous tippers to them as a special reward. He punished by lay-offs or by seating skinflints and fussy guests at an offender's table. All of this boiled up into a froth of vindictiveness which brought on every kind of foolishness, even in front of the customers.

The observation about the nature of waiters which André François Dupuis had communicated to Jack and me on his first visit to *La Garonne* defined his unalterable attitude toward them. However, he was content to live and let live, so long as the dishes prepared in his kitchen were picked up in good time and rushed to the proper table while still hot and bubbling, or chilled and glazed. On occasion, he would take over from a dilatory waiter and himself serve his dishes, subsequently immersing the offender in corrosive scorn. As for the rivalries among the waiters, he remained indifferent, until it became evident that such petty nonsense was delaying the delivery of dishes from the kitchen to the diners. After observing a *soufflé* collapse into a custard while the waiter responsible for serving it bickered with another in the kitchen doorway, he complained to Jack.

The following morning, a puzzled and apprehensive Dicky was summarily summoned to Jack's office. The message was brief and categoric: Dicky would use the Raid and get rid of the fruit flies or Jack himself would use it — and Dicky would share the fate of the insects.

16

From time to time, *La Garonne* did enjoy the services of exceptionally competent waiters, artists at their profession, who could dexterously bone a Dover sole, serve a tidy tower of sauteed baby potatoes by manipulating fork and spoon one-handed, or peel an orange on a fork in an unbroken serpentine of rind without touching a finger to it. Roger was one of these, a master who quietly and without ostentation added the touches that transform eating into dining. And then there was Flamin' 'Arry.

Harry was something else again, a natural born huckster with an irresistible pitch and a penchant for showmanship. He could have sold sand to Arabs. He did a great deal towards establishing *La Garonne's* notoriety as the most expensive restaurant in the state. It was one of his victims who remarked, "We decided not to have dinner at *La Garonne* and buy a color television instead."

A Bow Bells Englishman, Harry had thirty-five years' experience on land and sea as waiter, table captain, and *maître d'hotel.* He had been hired by Dicky as a combination dining room captain and personnel manager, with the right to tables of his own. Dicky was especially happy to have him, because Harry not only restored discipline in the dining rooms, but when he was at the restaurant, Dicky could leave whenever he wished, secure in the knowledge that things would run smoothly in his absence.

The management of the dining rooms didn't require much of Harry's attention during the evening, so he was able to give considerable expression to his unusual talent for merchandising food. Even as he was seating a party, he started applying soft soap, flattering the ladies with compliments and making solicitous inqueries about their comfort. He informed his patrons of their desire for cocktails, and whatever they chose, be it scotch with Coke, inevitably received his approval. Menus were presented with assurances of his readiness to assist in structuring the meal, a covert warning that *his* clientele would not deign to consider anything so prosaic as the *table d'hôte* dinner at a mere $6.50. Those who were incautious enough to ignore his hints to that effect found their meal poisoned by condescension and indifferent service. He was interested only in big spenders, and when necessary he was prepared to devote half the night and all his ingenuity to making prodigals out of pinchfists.

Pâté was a must after cocktails, or at the very least a half dozen *escargots* or, perhaps, melon with Italian ham. He never insisted on soups, because they were filling and might discourage an appetite for a dessert which cost four times as much. Unless his guests ordered *chateaubriand* for two, whose price alone guaranteed a substantial tip, he was disinclined to express enthusiasm for any dishes not "finished" by himself at the table. He knew his wines, and he promoted these *hors d'oeuvres* through dessert, insisting on their necessity and dictating their choice. Following reverential display of the label and the ceremony of presenting the cork and trial sip, he would lavish praise upon the guests for the subtlety of *their* selection.

He could have talked a gorged python into dessert. His favorites were *crêpes Suzette* and cherries jubilee, which he prepared, he modestly inferred, uniquely. Indeed he did, for no one poured on the V.S.O.P. cognac and Grand Marnier like Harry. Mere coffee was never satisfactory, and he introduced scores to the pleasures of his *café diable*, at the same time providing a spectacle which would have caused a fireman to blanch. In his passion for flaming everything, he turned his corner of the dining room into a shrine with a perpetual flame, kept alive by gallons of cognac and liqueurs. He even ignited dishes which needed no such treatment, or which suffered from it, for he had found the mystic rites in which he specialized were a sure means to bigger tips. Thus he spared neither fire nor spirits, dancing nimbly around the pillar of flame and sloshing on the liquor to prolong the display.

André François Dupuis did a slow burn himself when he found that Harry was flaming his carefully seasoned *ris de veau*, and he exploded at the realization that Harry's gallonage was being charged to the kitchen account, a matter of extreme sensitivity to any cost-conscious chef. He complained about this to the owners, since Dicky seemed unable or unwilling to stay Harry's liberal hand. In return, Harry charged that the chef was decrepit, that he resisted suggestions to revise the menu, and that he refused to cooperate with the dining room staff. As far as reducing food costs was concerned, in Harry's opinion the most obvious thing would be to fire the chef.

One night they had a real set to. Harry was serving a party of liberal spenders, and their appreciative response to his skill with chafing dish and combustibles suggested to his fertile mind that his gratuity would be even greater if he prepared a unique dessert, one not on the menu. His recommendation that they explore the delights of *bananes flambées* was greeted with tipsy approval, and he retired to the kitchen to assemble the ingredients. There he found that the supply of bananas had been exhausted, so he told the potwasher to run out and buy some at a nearby grocery which remained open until midnight. André François Dupuis overheard this order and countermanded it, insisting on his exclusive prerogative to determine what foods would be purchased and what would not. Harry's expostulations were to no avail, and Dicky could not be located to settle the issue, so Harry had to return to his table and communicate the sad tiding. The guests made do with *crêpes Suzette*, but this was little consolation to the disgruntled Harry, who felt that he had somehow lost face. When Dicky reappeared, Harry filled his ear and insisted the matter be reported to the owners, which it was. The whole hassel seemed rather petty to us, and we refused to take sides —which satisfied no one. The episode was noted, however, as an ominous portent that *La Garonne*, spacious as it was, was unlikely to be big enough to hold both Harry and Dupuis much longer.

17

André François Dupuis was in no sense ordinary. In his almost sixty years of life, he had not spared the flesh when the spirit had been willing, and it showed. He suffered from a variety of serious ailments, which he regarded as nuisances and for which he took pills only because it would have been painful, or even fatal, not to. A partial loss of balance caused an occasional stagger, hinting at the "long tongue" peculiar to his profession, but he had no interest in alcohol. Forced by his mutinous organs to a life of watchful moderation, he had become a philosopher of sorts, seeking life's answers in books and conversation. He was basically kind hearted and sentimental, but his cruel apprenticeship in France under brutal *sous-chefs* and later experiences in the school of hard knocks had made him mistrustful and uncompromising. In the kitchen, he was a dictator, an aging lion whose authority was maintained by power of personality and a palpable menace of physical violence.

He got along well with Dicky, for whom he developed a fatherly affection. Although he instantly recognized Dicky's shortcomings as a manager, he was determined that he could make him effective in the position he occupied. He revealed to Dicky the astonishing ways that certain employees were stealing from the restaurant or at least getting something for nothing. He made Dicky enforce the rule that time-cards not be punched until the waiters were dressed and ready for work, rather than when they arrived for their meals. He caught the worst pilferers red-handed and stood over Dicky until he summoned the fortitude to fire them. And he thought that his protégé was making progress, for Dicky did not resist his advice, quite affably taking criticism, acceding to suggestions, even putting new rules and procedures into operation. But nothing really changed, for the transformation was entirely superficial. Dicky would agree with anyone on anything, perhaps even at the moment convinced of his own sincerity.

Dicky was kind to André François Dupuis, driving him to the restaurant every morning and seeing that he was taken home at night. He affected an interest in the chef's philosophical inquiries, and would listen by the hour to his rambling discourse. Dicky would run to the drugstore for his pills, mail his letters, chauffeur him places, and in general he made the chef's life comfortable and serene. When the chef had a falling out with the *saucier* and the cook-butcher, Dicky encouraged him to fly to Florida to recruit replacements, incidentally booking him into the most opulent of Gold Coast hotels. Meanwhile, he bribed the pair to stay on at *La Garonne* with an extra fifty dollars a week under the table.

The happy relationship between the chef and Dicky began to deteriorate with the arrival of Flamin' 'Arry. To enjoy the easier life that Harry's presence made possible, Dicky had to make sure that the Englishman would remain at *La Garonne*, arranging that his employment was pleasurable and profitable. The profit aspect he managed with raises and gifts of the restaurant's appurtenances for Harry's apartment, but he could not make life pleasant for him so long as Dupuis remained chef. In trying to appease both parties, he invariably offended one or the other. André François

Dupuis was not about to accept less than total loyalty, and his opinion of Dicky was increasingly eroded with each new favor accorded Harry.

The antagonism between Harry and Dupuis added another dimension to the owners' relationships. After Hughes was no longer with us, the investors more or less resumed their original cordiality. Ricardo toned down his criticism of Dicky, at least at our meetings, and Ralph and Willis took comfort in the fact that the rest of us, although far from satisfied, seemed resigned to the *status quo*. Dupuis' initial support of Dicky and his expectations of making him over into a real manager not only strengthened Dicky's position but caused Ralph and Willis to regard the chef in a very favorable light. But then Harry appeared, and positions and postures began to change. Harry knew how to ingratiate himself and he had talent, so our opinion of him was unanimously positive. Once he started feuding with the chef, he lost my vote, but he gradually won over Ralph and Willis as Dicky gravitated from Dupuis' orbit to that of Harry. The rearrangement of alliances was further accelerated by rising labor costs in the kitchen, where the chef had justified an increase in staff owing to expanded volume of business. The gross was rising, but we had still to make our first penny of profit. Jack and I remained doggedly optimistic, but Eric, Dwight, and Ricardo were increasingly souring on Dupuis as he proved unable to produce the promised pie in the sky. They also had the impression, cautiously insinuated by Harry, that *La Garonne* might prosper if both the chef and the manager were replaced, the chef by a younger and less expensive man and the manager by you-know-who.

Such was the balance of power, obviously too delicate to endure. Someone or something had to fall.

18

The crystal chandeliers, sparkling glasses, gleaming silver, brilliant linen, deferential waiters and soft music all combined to produce an atmosphere of genteel decorum in the dining rooms. In deference to this aura, the customers progressively lowered their voices as they proceeded from the area of the checkroom through the foyer toward the salon. Any raucous laughter, too animated conversation, or, heaven forfend, disputatious tones, would bring forth admonitory frowns from the waiters and even a visit by the captain, who would never criticize but rather would dispel too gay a mood by breaking in with polite questions about the meal or the service.

One busy night, the customary tranquility of *La Garonne's* main salon was shatteringly smashed by an hysterical, "My God, a BAT. My hair!" A cry of "Fire!" could hardly have caused such a reaction. High pitched "Eeeks" and cries of "where, where is it?" sparked across the tables, glasses were overturned and silver sent flying as the ladies, especially those coiffed *à la* bee hive, snatched for their napkins or even the tablecloth itself to snood their hair. Meanwhile, the apparent cause of the outrage disappeared, leaving the salon in a state of apprehension more cruel than the odious presence itself. The tension somewhat abated, permitting the escort of the lady who had sounded the alarm to express his doubts as to her mental health.

"Look, you were the only person to see it. If there were a bat, don't you think someone else would have seen it?"

"There was a bat. Don't look at me as if I were crazy. And for God's sake lower your voice."

"I didn't do the screaming. Just calm down. Probably you saw a shadow or some movement in the corner of your eye."

"Don't try to tell me what I saw. I saw a bat."

"Well, it's sort of dark in here and . . ."

"I don't care how dark it is. I know a bat when I see one. There was a bat in here. And if it comes back, I'm leaving!"

Tolerantly. "That's just fine. We won't worry any more about it. If you did see something, it's probably gone away. Now, as I was saying before your little scene . . ."

At this moment, like breakers running onto a beach, a series of "Eeeks" swept across the dining room as the creature reappeared and circled the room, then disappeared through the velvet curtained doorway connecting the main salon with the smaller dining room. Its unwanted presence there was immediately signaled by a chorus of shrieks and the sound of breaking glass. The waiters in the larger room ran towards the commotion only to recoil against one another as the furry visitor swooped back through the opening, banked to avoid the grand chandelier, and headed for the foyer. Someone with great presence of mind yelled, "Get a tennis racquet!" probably recalling an old home remedy for such invasions. As the rodent-bird fluttered into the foyer, there was a collective sigh of relief, followed by a collective gasp of horror as it reappeared. The bat then began flying laps around the salon, using the smaller chandeliers at the end of the room as pylons, altering its flight plan only to outwit the more venturesome waiters who flapped at it with napkins as it passed over them. The humor of the situation was not obvious to those directly beneath the creature's recurring pattern, and they cringed as it swept over them and raised their hands in terror of an expected plunge into their hair. The commotion increased and word of the uninvited guest was conveyed to the kitchen, bringing forth the white garbed André François Dupuis. From the service area, he impassively observed the scene, his cod-like eyes betraying no reaction. To some, his stolid figure and emotional calm suggested him as a savior, and voices implored him to "Do something!" as if he could simply pop the bat into a pot like a lobster. He answered their entreaties with a Gallic shrug and vanished back into the kitchen.

The bat, irritated by the hostile reception and the lashing napkins, now added further horror to its presence by squeaking harshly, a sound akin to that of fingernails dragged across a blackboard. Its cries seemed to call for others of its kind to join it, and the more imaginative guests heard replies from the dark shadows of the potted palms and the folds of the velvet drapes. The diners began to give indications of a mass exodus, and Dicky knew that on this occasion no gift of wine would persuade them to stay. His troops, too, seemed on the verge of a rout, and in a desperate effort to capture the beast, he mustered his panicked force into a group at the end of the room, thereby concentrating their lashing power. With derisive shrieks, the bat avoided the linen ack-ack and continued on its mission, circling the room with terrifying single-mindedness. Flamin' 'Arry, who had courageously protected the contents of his chafing dish throughout the attack, now sought to burn the enemy in flight by creating a pillar of flame as it approached. The ceiling showed the effects instantly, but the offender escaped unscathed. Everyone was ready to bolt, but no one dared risk the hazardous path to freedom. Just as the anguish and desperation reached the point of mass derangement, André François Dupuis reappeared from the kitchen, a giant balloon whisk grasped firmly in hand. Almost before anyone was aware of his return, he took a lightning cut at the fluttering pest, knocking it back into the service area, where it fell into the cashier's slot at Nicky's feet.

Throughout the contest, Nicky had been cringing beside his register, his pallor and hands serving as an instrument for measuring the bat's proximity, for he would blanch as the creature sped towards his end of the dining room, involuntarily thrusting his palms in its direction to ward off attack. Now, with the stunned creature quivering at his feet, his terror was boundless. He gave forth an animal cry and sprang out into the dining room, turning in mid-air to maintain his observation of the bat. His next Nureyevian spring carried him to the doorway joining the two rooms, and there he paused to measure the distance between himself and the menacing monster. This dramatic performance broke the spell of horror, and the dining room was racked by relieved laughter.

Meanwhile, the resourceful chef enveloped the bat in a towel and, with a glance of total disdain in the direction of the shuddering Nicky, he plodded back to his kitchen.

Brandy sales hit an all time high that evening.

19

Restaurants are an ideal target for complaints, for it is true that there is no accounting for tastes. *La Garonne* had its share of disgruntled customers, especially during the weeks when Dicky and his band occupied the kitchen. André François Dupuis did much to erase that charred image, but he was not immune to criticism himself, particularly from gourmet purists whose expectations were deceived by his capricious variations of dishes bearing traditional titles. His *canard à l'orange*, for example, was garnished with pineapple, not orange wedges, and the sauce was an unexpected reddish color. Excellent in its own right, it was not strictly *classique*. Occasionally a particularly knowledgeable guest took note of the absence of mussels in the *filet de sole Marguery*, and the chef's *coq au vin Chambertin* should have been billed simply as *coq au vin rouge*, which would have avoided problems from those guests who could tell *Chambertin* from *rouge ordinaire*. At times, he was overly generous with the garlic in his *scampi La Garonne*, which didn't cause objections from the person eating it but did offend those with whom he shared the table, who choked and wept as their lethal companion enveloped them in palpable clouds of essence.

The service also came in for criticism, because it was impossible to have an entire meal served in less than three hours. It took longer if the waiter did a boo-hoo on the back stairs. The preparation of the salad alone required a minimum of thirty minutes, and involved numerous trips to the buffet for mustard, salt, oil, vinegar, and the pepper mill, all of which had to be meticulously arranged before the garlicking of the bowl began. This act was properly performed by holding the clove between wooden fork and spoon, a trick within the talent of but few of the waiters. The less talented were determined nonetheless, and by the quarter hour they would chase the pesky clove around the bowl, sometimes sending it ricochetting off into the dining room. When the dressing was finally made, it was allowed to meld while greens were brought from the cooler. Presented at the table in a damp napkin, they were then placed tenderly into the salad bowl. The tossing of the lettuce was a ticklish process, so that no leaf would be bruised and each would have its share of the dressing. The serving of the salad onto chilled plates (another trip to the kitchen was needed to procure these) was done with elaborate concern for the location of each bit of greenery. Concert or theatre goers, anxious to have a quick meal before a performance, were known to have suffered psychological trauma from the salad ritual. One was better advised to forget about his tickets, since even a rush effort was not likely to produce a complete repast before the final curtain.

The menu itself provoked negative comment, since it was beyond the joint capabilities of the chef and the printer to produce a copy without several dozen spelling errors. Accents were scattered randomly, as if applied with a pepper mill, and *meunière* would appear correctly on one line and as *meneré* the next. *Hélène* lost her "H" and her accents, but an extra letter might be added to *entrecôte* to produce *entrecôtte*. *Rijsttafel*, which the chef included in memory of his days in Amsterdam, was presented as *Ridstaffel*, and there was a polyglot's delight in *"Prosciutto avec Melon in season."* *La Garonne* received a great deal of mail on this matter from students of Elementary French at the university.

The prices reaped the most constant harvest of complaints, for even a modest dinner cost more than the Huronese were accustomed or willing to pay. If, in a moment of fiscal aberration, one dared go beyond the limits of the *table d'hôte* dinner, he risked instant impoverishment. An *à la carte* dinner of *pâté*, turtle soup, green salad, *tournedos Rossini*, with asparagus *hollandaise*, followed by *patisserie* and coffee, produced a bill of $15, even without cocktails or wine. Those who fell victim to the blandishments of Flamin' 'Arry had prodigious checks. However, their complaints were usually deferred, because when Harry structured a meal his customers were anesthetized beyond the point of pain long before the bill arrived.

Our most amusing episode of customer dissatisfaction was a multiple complaint not only about the food, the service, and the prices but also about a surprise shower. Owing to a quirk inherent in our building, periodically there was a cascade of murky waters from the ceiling of the smaller dining room onto the patrons below. We knew this recurring deluge had something to do with the antique heating registers on the second floor, but no plumber was ever able to find the source. Through experience, we learned that by draining the boiler we could obtain symptomatic relief, but this required appointing a volunteer to crawl into a remote catacomb of the basement and open the appropriate valve, meanwhile taking his scalding like a man.

The sight of sedate diners suddenly showered with hot rusty water always provided an entertaining spectacle for those beyond harm's way, and the victims, once removed to a dry table and provided restitution in the form of free drinks and wine, usually ended by laughing at their experience. One night, the show was particularly fascinating because the target table was occupied by a French couple, a stick-like little man and his beefy, moustachiod spouse. From the moment of their arrival, they had expressed annoyance with various aspects of the food and service and had carped about the prices. Dicky had been made aware of their hostile attitude and was lurking in the wings with his propitiatory wines when the sound of scraping chairs and an irate *"Mon Dieu!"* signaled the worst. A quick check confirmed his apprehension that the diners had fallen prey to the unpredictable Niagara, and he rushed to the main salon to get Harry.

At that moment, Harry was engaged in the rites of *café diable* and disinclined to leave his pyre, but Dicky's frantic gestures finally prevailed. They held a hasty conference in the service area.

"Harry, for God's sake, the ceiling's flooding again. You've got to go down and drain the boiler."

"In a pig's eye, I will. Last time I made that trip I got me arse burned. Not this time. You send Wally, 'e don't know the meaning of fear."

Wally, a recent employee who was ignorant of the peril involved, was duly instructed in the procedure of draining down the boiler. While he parboiled like a lobster in the tomb below, the cascade abated. Meanwhile, other waiters had solicitously moved the sodden couple to a new table and they had calmed sufficiently to encourage Dicky's approach. He apologized profusely for the unfortunate incident, and then remarked that he hoped everything else had been all right. That was an error.

"Wha to you meen, all ride? Eez it all ride when I ordaire *Martini* for somsing to serve weez chin? Zat eez not French *Martini*. And wha teez weez zee *pâté maison?* Zat eez nod from zeez maison but from zee box. And wha teez weez ze *vin,* zat eez more *vinaigre* zan *vin?* And wha teez weez zee prize of zeez *vinaigre* at four dollar? *Finalement,*" and his voice rose shrilly — to the added joy of his enchanted audience — "*Finalement,* wha teez weez zeez plaz zat we ordaire ze *diner* but we get ze *douche?*" And out they stalked.

None of us complained when Dicky charged their unpaid check to "Account 999," although "Promotion of Business" hardly seemed an appropriate designation for the incident.

20

The misbehavior of the antique heating registers was not the only source of dark humor at *La Garonne*, for we possessed numerous pieces of ancient equipment with the capacity for original and amusing antics. One of these relics was the device which turned on the outside light to illuminate the facade. This whimsical engine would unaccountably shut off at darkness and resume its labors at dawn, thus providing Huron's main thoroughfare with supplementary lighting during the daylight hours. The ice machine was another temperamental item, and it always was most productive from Sunday through Wednesday, in its zeal even spilling its product onto the floor. But as the weekend approached, and vast quantities of ice were needed for the bar and dining rooms, it would sigh and quit, at the same time contriving to melt the fruits of its Sunday to Wednesday efforts.

The worst offender, the air-conditioning plant, was new to the premises, but no less ancient than its mechanical companions. With an uncharacteristic concern for economy, Dicky had bought it second (?) hand for next to nothing in some remote corner of the state, and then paid a small fortune to have it trucked to Huron. It should rather have gone to the Smithsonian's display of early American machinery. Its many parts were installed in various places about the restaurant where space could be found, and a team of specialists was assembled to get it running. Every time it began to gasp encouragingly and they started to pack up their tools, it would hiccup and clank into immobility. Weeks were spent trying to keep its fans turning, and all this preceded the production of even a puff of cold air. When it finally did run at its asthmatic best, it kept the place tolerably cool, but it regularly relapsed in a neurotic effort to attract attention. This singular machine had one odd feature which no artisan of whatever expertise could correct. If it were turned on without opening a certain valve, immediately the whole service area between the main dining room and the kitchen would flood, displacing our Parisian effect with one more suited to Venice. Without gondolas, the waiters were obliged to wade until the waters receded.

Such antediluvian apparatus naturally harmonized nicely with the general decrepitude of those areas of *La Garonne* which were not open to the public. Not even the miles of new water lines and wiring, distribution panels, circuit breakers, and fuse boxes which we installed, or even the new boiler and hot water heater, could alleviate the aura of dilapidation which prevailed throughout the second floor and in the basement. And it was this condition that encouraged inspectors of all kinds to find our establishment ideally suited to the exercise of their profession.

Inspectors were a plague to our restaurant and thrice damned with each visit. We had thought that we had satisfied the stringent demands of fire, building, electrical, plumbing, and sundry other inspectors at the time we were first permitted to open our doors. But such was not the case, for these guardians of public safety continued to reappear. Each new visit would impose the necessity of adding new extinguishers, fire doors, and "EXIT" lights, along with more orders to remove old wiring, burst pipes, cracked sinks, disconnected toilets, and other junk from the unused second floor or basement. A truck load of trash might be hauled away to satisfy the decrees of a particular inspector, but when he or a colleague appeared, subsequently another load would have materialized. It were as though the impedimenta were actually breeding in the dark recesses of the old candy kitchen or the basement catacombs.

The sanitation and health inspectors had more justification, for the place not only conveyed the impression of being dirty — it was. Before the restaurant opened, we had made uncommon expenditures of money and effort to satisfy their demands, not to speak of our own desires, that the *Sanitation Code* be implemented. Fans, screens, filters, dispensors had been installed, and a supermarket's supply of soaps, detergents, cleansing powders, acids, ammonias, and rinsing agents had been purchased for the maintenance of sanitary conditions. On the night preceding the first preview dinner, the owners and their wives had joined forces with Dicky's crew to give the kitchen and dining areas a final cleaning, an effort which concluded after dawn. From then on it was all downhill, notwithstanding the purchase of an enormous steam cleaner, which remained neglected in the basement. Monsieur Renault had coasted along on this initial cleaning, paying attention only to the work areas and passageways in the kitchen. During the interregnum when Dicky and his volunteers did the cooking, there was an acceleration of deterioration. André François Dupuis made an effort to reestablish order and sanitation, but no amount of threats and dismissals could force his itinerant cleaning staff to sweep the broken crockery from under the counters or get after the sprouting onions and potatoes which had fallen into hard-to-reach places. And, understandably, no one was interested in fishing for the trout heads or scrod tails which the oblivious cook-butcher kept kicking under his counter. The chef was also impotent when it came to getting the night porter to carry out the garbage when he cleaned the kitchen, and regularly after closing on Saturday night great cans of liquifying offal stood quietly fermenting in the warm kitchen until the chef's arrival Monday morning.

The walk-in iceboxes, coolers, and freezers were ominous cells suggestive of the charnel houses of a past era. Damp, peeling, and rusty, it is a wonder they ever got past the inspectors — yet they did. In view of such obvious hazards to health, it is paradoxical that *La Garonne* was most frequently cited for violation of the *Sanitation Code* because of our failure to remove an antique ice cream machine located in a remote chamber of the basement. In the days when *The Coffee Spoon* had been a confectionery and soda fountain, the machine had doubtless done yeoman duty, but its days of labor had forever passed. Merely a shell of its former self, without innards and accessories, its refrigeration lines had been disconnected and the electric wires to its motor had been removed. But each succeeding inspector made it his personal crusade to have it removed.

"You guys gotta get rid of this machine. You know better than to prepare food in a basement like this. Jeez, that's an old bugger!"

Patiently. "We don't use it, we have never used it, we don't intend to use it, and we couldn't if we wanted to. There's no electricity connected to it, and there's no way to make it freeze. How can we possibly use it?"

"Look. I'm here to protect the public. The code says you can't prepare food in a storage basement. You guys just won't get that through your heads. It's against the law to make ice cream in this basement. Now you've gotta get this machine out of here right away. We've tried to be nice about this and give you guys a break, but this is the third time we've told you and you gotta do something about it. Christ, it'ud make you sick to think of eating anything made in that old thing. I don't see how you guys stomach it."

"Now, inspector, please listen. We run a French restaurant. What little ice cream we use we buy from the dairy. I can show you in the freezer upstairs the ice cream from the dairy. We just don't use this machine and wouldn't if we could. It hasn't worked for years, you can see for yourself."

"Yeh, I know, I've heard it before. I don't want you to take this personal, I'm just doing my job. The law says no food preparation in unsanitary conditions. Look around you, jeez, this is a hell of a place to fix food for people to eat."

"All right. We'll take it out; we'll get rid of it. We promise not to use it until we can get it taken away. Just give us a couple of days."

"O.K. I'm with you. You don't use it and you get it out of here right away."

But we never did.

21

The last straw is always just that, some relatively insignificant item which assumes disproportionate weight because the breaking point has been reached. Dicky's downfall came about in just such circumstances.

One fine day in late summer, Jack received a letter threatening a lawsuit unless the corporation immediately paid $1,250 promised by Dicky for some carpentry work performed during the renovation period. The correspondent also included a bill for six etchings, which he claimed had been purchased from him at $50 each to decorate the restaurant. In conclusion, he noted that he had been waiting almost a year for his money and that Dicky simply ignored his letters demanding payment. All of this was news to Jack, as well as the rest of us, and it couldn't have come at a worse time for Dicky.

With Hughes' withdrawal from our enterprise, I had reluctantly agreed to assume one aspect of his financial watchdog activity, the handling of accounts payable. To this melancholy task I added a mission of my own, the projection of a realistic operating budget. The accomplishment of both tasks required that I pry from Dicky a full disclosure of the commitments he had made, and was still making, in the corporation's name. The additional — and unsuspected — indebtedness revealed at that time was enormous, in particular with respect to advertising. For that item there was a batch of unpaid bills and contracts going back even to the period of our opening.

To avoid criticism, and likely veto of expenditures, Dicky had quietly withheld the billings from the accountant, hoping that later profits would cover the expense, if not justify it. In any case, the name of *La Garonne*, accompanied by his own as Manager, either had already appeared or was scheduled to appear in every conceivable trade and professional journal, in theatre programs and yearbooks, in entertainment guides and advertising blotters, not to mention large cuts in newspapers and spot announcements on the radio. His "full" disclosure at that time even revealed that *La Garonne* was sponsoring a program of dinner music on an obscure FM channel.

To cover the most urgent of these accumulated bills, I had to dun each of the investors for another $3,000. Needless to say, they parted with their money reluctantly, and in some cases profanely. In the following weeks, Dicky continued to swear that he really had disclosed every debt or contract, yet past due charges still kept trickling in, each "positively the last." There was no end of them.

A few days before Jack had received the letter demanding the $1,250, Dicky had nonchalantly presented me with an official notification from the state that *La Garonne* had failed to remit sales tax for several months running. The amount owed was almost $4,000. The notice itself was accompanied by copies of previously sent overdue warnings and schedules of punitive penalties. Also it seemed that our liquor license was about to be yanked because of our failure to turn over our tax. To arrange immediate payment, I was forced to draw on the funds set aside for the next payroll, and Jack, as the corporation's lawyer, had to provide an official explanation of our laxity. At the same time, he did what was necessary to reverse the license removal procedures. Dicky regarded the whole matter with the maddening insouciance of the true deadbeat.

Against the background of this sales tax matter and the problems it had caused, the disclosure of yet another overlooked debt brought on a violent reaction. Jack was rabid when he called me to find out if I knew anything about the $1,250, and he actually began frothing through the phone when he learned that the whole matter was news to me. I did a slow burn myself, one of many in recent weeks, because it was finally obvious that Dicky was being deliberately deceptive about our bills in order to avoid censure and to keep our dismal financial picture from looking hopeless. Yet it really wasn't the unpaid $1,250 which was the last straw for Jack and myself — it was the damn etchings.

Jack wouldn't hear of waiting until the regular Wednesday meeting. He wanted to pull the tooth and pull it now, whatever the pain. However, his ire didn't prevent him from realizing that Ralph and Willis would continue to support Dicky whatever happened, so, in preparation for the extraction, he suggested that Dwight, Eric, and I meet with him that evening to plan our strategy. Ricardo was out of town, but he could be counted on to support any anti-Dicky decision we might make.

As we discussed the situation in Dwight's cozy study, we were unreservedly unanimous that Dicky must go. The real problem was to find a replacement, and none of us had any brilliant insights in that regard. As we talked, our anti-Dicky animosities fed on one another, and before long we concluded that Dicky should be given the boot that night. At that point, Dwight suggested we invite Willis to join us, for, if we could convince him to go along with our decision, he would be able to work on Ralph. The idea of dumping Dicky, we reasoned, would definitely be more palatable to Ralph if it were broached by Willis than by one of us. A telephone call found Willis at home; he would be happy to come over.

When he arrived, Dwight first gave him a stiff drink to ease the pain of what was to follow. Jack then filled him in on the contents of the latest dunning letter, and I provided the gruesome details of futile efforts to extract information about creditors from our reticent manager. Jack followed my litany for a while and then burst in.

"We've put up with this foolishness for long enough. In the past month, I've been receiving calls every day from creditors we've never heard of. We haven't the foggiest idea of how much we're losing, except that we've exhausted our line of credit three times and every couple of weeks, we have to kick in another couple of thousand dollars apiece. And now this damn letter and these damn etchings are the end. The party's over; Dicky has got to go — now!"

There were murmurs of assent from the rest of us. Willis, who had listened with sober attention, now assumed an ingenuous expression. "I agree it looks bad, but Dicky should get a chance to explain. Maybe there's some misunderstanding."

Eric's response was more than emphatic. "What's to explain? So he comes here and gives us more of his la-de-da excuses, so what? We've been that route before. We just can't trust the guy. Dicky's out, I mean out, *O U T.*"

Willis wasn't convinced. "Maybe you're right, but Ralph is going to have something to say about it. So if you want to vote on it tonight, Ralph will have to be here."

The idea did not appeal to Jack. "We can vote next Wednesday to make it official. You know what Ralph's reaction will be. If he comes over now he'll be outvoted anyway." Willis shook his head negatively. Jack modified his approach. "If you think we can get ahold of him, fine. I suppose we may as well wash all the linen tonight as later."

While Dwight used the phone upstairs, the rest of us, for Willis's edification, engaged in a "Can you top this?" exposé of Dicky's prodigalities and prevarications. Dwight returned with the report that he had contacted Ralph at the restaurant and that he would be over shortly. The evening promised to become more interesting.

When Ralph arrived, jauntily attired as always, his anticipatory smile revealed that Dwight had not chosen to inform him over the phone about the nature of the business at hand. Sensing the tension, his smile faded, and he remained noncommittal while Dwight got him a drink and Jack summarized the situation. Surprisingly, Ralph agreed that Dicky had been something less than a managerial wizard. But having doffed his hat to that idea, he laid it on the line to the rest of us.

"You all get together here in some sort of star chamber and put the full blame on Dicky. We have a regular meeting time, and that's when this should be discussed, not on fifteen minutes' notice. And Dicky should be present. He's made mistakes, and so have you. Now you want to throw him out because of this letter without even asking for his side of it. And I suppose you have another manager in mind?"

Eric provided the answer. "No manager would be better. At least then we could finally find out what we owe. We haven't had a financial report in three months, and no one knows where we stand. But we do know one thing. There isn't enough in the bank to cover the next payroll, and that means another assessment. But just count me out on that score while Dicky stays."

Ralph was livid. "The payroll isn't Dicky's fault. You had to hire that Dupuis, and he's $400 a week. In my book he's no better than Renault at half the price. He's got the kitchen filled with people, and he's bad-mouthing Dicky and fighting with Harry. For my money, get rid of *him*. That's how to cut expenses. When he's gone, Dicky can do his job. But not while that s.o.b. is in the kitchen causing trouble."

Ralph's idea appealed to Eric. "Fine. I agree. Get rid of Dicky *and* Dupuis. Kill two birds with one stone. Dicky's spending too much and Dupuis costs too much."

Jack was not about to be red-herringed with talk of firing the chef. "Dupuis is a separate issue. Now, Ralph, if *you* want to see Dicky stay and *you* want to fire Dupuis, go right ahead. You have my vote. But then *you* find the money to cover the payroll, and *you* take care of the accounts payable, and I'll just have all the creditors' calls switched to your office."

Ralph became shrill. "Don't try to saddle me with your mistakes. Ever since we started, you and your east side Mafia have done just what you damn well pleased. You've been on Dicky's neck from the start, right along with Ricardo and Hughes. Now you want a scapegoat. Not one of you knows enough to run a business by himself."

This last gratuitous remark was happily drowned out in the rising tide of angry rebuttals precipitated by his previous comments. I was the only one who heard it, and I chose to ignore its relevance to myself. Besides, Dwight's study was far too nice to become an abattoir.

The argument flared and waned for over an hour, group therapy at its wildest. When all the personal abuse up to the limits of physical attack had been vented, the atmosphere cooled a bit and some proposals began to be discussed. A grudging compromise, which left everyone dissatisfied, was the result. Dicky would be relieved as manager but allowed to remain as *maître d'hotel*. The accountant would be replaced and a complete financial report prepared on a crash program. A junta consisting of Dwight, Eric, and myself would take charge until a new manager could be found, and Jack would continue to temporize with the creditors.

The next morning, Dwight located Dicky and explained the situation to him. Dicky's lack of surprise indicated that the previous night's festivities were not unknown to him. While he removed his personal effects from the restaurant office, the accounting task force, assembled by Eric, arrived. The chef, Harry, and the head bartender were summoned and admonished to cooperate or else, and each was made responsible for his immediate staff. When the waiters arrived, they were informed that the era of fun-and-games was over.

Eric was very effective in conveying his latter message, his serious manner made particularly emphatic by his obvious physical ability to handle any, or all, malefactors. In fact, he scared the hell out of them.

Our digging through the restaurant's office and files opened a can of worms. More contracts for promotional services turned up, plus exasperated letters from creditors who had never been mentioned. We discovered that Dicky, without a word to Jack or myself, had hired his brother as assistant manager. There were citations from the local health and safety authorities categorically threatening to padlock the place unless certain conditions were corrected, and these bore the ominous stamp "Final Notification." Finance companies with chattel mortgages on equipment promised immediate repossession unless payments were brought up to date. Among the papers which Dicky left behind was an IBM printout from the police department listing over fifty of his parking violations, not for expired meters but for blocking driveways, parking in front of hydrants, and occupying loading zones. A mimeographed letter announced someone's appointment to membership in *The Marching Society* and *Daisy Chain*. There was a florist's bill charged to *La Garonne* for eighteen long-stemmed red roses. The order carbon, which was stapled to the bill, called for the roses to be accompanied by a card, the tender message of which was on the order, and delivered — to a man.

All of this was too much. The junta wanted Dicky out and told him so.

He left quietly.

22

The new accountant and his cohorts launched themselves into their task with the eagerness of the Internal Revenue Service enjoying the windfall of a mobster's business ledgers. In the webby grime of the basement, under light provided by a naked bulb, they sorted and arranged, jotted and totalled, checked and cross-checked, trying to fit together the financial picture from heaps of bills, invoices, register tapes, deposit slips, cancelled checks, pay-roll accounts, contracts, and an autumn harvest of random slips of paper on which Dicky, with rare conscientiousness, had noted various amounts withdrawn from the cash registers for "Paid Outs." Among these was evidence of salary advances to persons who had never put in an hour's labor, as well as an answer to how Dicky's marathon parking violations had been supported.

The accountant's report was ready within a week. Our corporate disposition, although rather testy, had improved some-what with Dicky finally out of the picture, so everyone was agree-able to a luncheon meeting at a private club for the purpose of hearing the accountant's findings. As we nibbled at our salads, the accountant passed around copies of his financial statement and then took the floor. He led off with some general remarks, mentioning that food costs were high but possibly within reason for the kind of restaurant involved, that liquor costs were a few points higher than for a typical bar operation, but at least there seemed to be profit in that area. On hearing this better-than-anticipated news, we relaxed a little. Then came the bombshell. Labor costs were "beyond comprehension," and when coupled with cost of sales, the total was over 120% of our gross. With great consideration, he gently added that this was exclusive of general overhead, such as rent, depreciation, utilities, debt retirement, advertising and insurance.

While we pondered this in stunned silence, the main course was served, and after the waitress withdrew, the accountant continued. Renovation and start-up costs were in excess of $125,000 and the operating loss to date exceeded $60,000. Assuming an average check of $10 per person and correlating this with gross receipts, the owners had been subsidizing each dinner by over two dollars. The accountant then tactfully pointed out that perhaps our operation, given the kind of food and service it required, lacked sufficient seating capacity to produce a profit even with full utilization of the premises and good management. While we stared at our plates, he turned to his steak.

Faced with objective proof of our deplorable performance as restaurateurs and investors, we mulled the alternatives. One seemed obvious, and we unanimously agreed — dump the white elephant at the first opportunity. There was a feeling, which the accountant supported, that live elephants sell better than dead ones, so we decided, but without enthusiasm, to keep *La Garonne* open until we had a reasonable offer. As it happens, no one makes reasonable offers for dying elephants.

The three of us who formed the managerial junta faced our chore with joyless determination, conscious that even our best efforts might do little more than prolong the agonies of our moribund beast. The first order of business was to slash our labor costs, and here we found Harry, whom we had put in charge of everything to do with the dining rooms, and the bartender, an aimiable Burmese named Thatch, more pliable than André François Dupuis. The waiter staff on week nights was trimmed, the coat check girl eliminated, the parking attendant taken off salary and put on an hourly rate for weekends only, and the second bartender reduced from full time to Fridays and Saturdays. These changes were a step in the right direction, but they saved less than $250 a week.

The kitchen offered real possibilities for economy, for labor there was in excess of $1,400 a week, not counting what the cook-butcher and *saucier* were receiving under the table. At this time, the chefdom of André François Dupuis included nine employees, for besides the original staff of *saucier*, cook-butcher, *garde-mangé*, dishwasher and potwasher, there was now a broiler man, an extra dishwasher on weekends, and a utility employee who cleaned and did odd chores. The desperate financial condition was candidly outlined to the chef, who was sympathetic but disinclined to reduce his staff in view of the general increase in business. The *saucier*, Rudolph, whom Dupuis invariably characterized as "that moron," was indispensable, as was the broiler man. However, the cook-butcher might be sacrificed. He was lazy and a "loud mouth" and had been retained only out of fear that if he left he would take his crony, the moronic Rudolph, with him. According to the chef, a recent quarrel between loud mouth and the moron had eliminated that menace, a piece of information which we would have enjoyed learning sooner. The potwasher could also go, since the utility man had been doing most of his work anyhow. So an additional $300 a week was pared off kitchen salaries.

Among ourselves, Dwight, Eric, and I discussed the obvious economy of eliminating André François Dupuis, since for some time it had been clear that the chef's poor health had made him quite unable to handle any of the heavier or hotter jobs behind the stoves. Rudolph had been carrying on in place of the chef, acting as a pair of hands responsive to the will of the older man. Another $300 a week could easily be saved by replacing them both with a less expensive chef capable of directing the kitchen and functioning as *saucier*. The theory was attractive, but its realization seemed doubtful on the basis of our earlier experience in seeking a chef, not to mention the total failure of the Florida foray to produce a single applicant. There were other considerations, such as the cold-bloodedness of dismissing an ailing retainer, and there was also no denying that *La Garonne's* widening reputation was not independent of the name of André François Dupuis.

Of course, more capital was needed to continue under any circumstances, for without money to temporize with the creditors, supplies would be cut off and the premises stripped bare. Jack, whose offices were under seige by creditors, was barely able to keep us an hour ahead of involuntary bankruptcy, and he had to pay purveyors cash before they would unload supplies. A final extension of $30,000 credit was arranged, to be supplemented by additional contributions from the owners. Most squeaked plaintively and came up with the required amount, but Ricardo reluctantly had to call it quits.

23

While we were losing money even faster than the most pessimistic of us imagined, our acquaintances assumed that *La Garonne* was just naturally a gold mine. One of them raised the subject with me in the bar on a certain evening.

"You guys got it made. You're charging a buck twenty-five for a martini, and it isn't even made with Beefeater. That's over thirty bucks profit for every bottle. Some business."

I smiled indulgently. "A good business to stay out of. First of all, you're wrong, because we give two ounces of gin in our martinis and then add the vermouth, so that's less than seventeen dollars we take in for each bottle, and the bottle costs us over four dollars."

"Well and good, but you still make a sweet net of thirteen bucks on each bottle."

"Net isn't exactly the right word. Look at your drink and tell me what you see."

"Well, there's the martini, the olive, and the ice."

"What about the toothpick and the napkin under the glass?"

"Big deal. I'm bleeding for you on the toothpicks."

"And what do you see on the bar?"

"Some nuts, cheese and crackers, and other drinks."

"Right, and those other drinks require oranges, cherries, limes, pineapple, onions, bitters, sugar, syrup, lemon and orange juice, and they all cost money."

"Come on, that's hardly a drop in the bucket."

"Well, fresh fruit doesn't come cheap, and we have to keep eggs and cream on hand for fizzes and Alexanders. Then there's the mixes, soda, ginger, quinine, naturally Schweppes."

"Bring me my violin."

"I've just started. What about the bartender's salary, his assistant, the hat check girl, the cocktail waitress, the piano player, and don't forget the people who clean the place or service the equipment. There's even a little man who comes twice a month to wash out the beer spigots and clean the lines to the kegs. His little visit costs twenty-four dollars."

"You've forgotten rent and utilities," my friend volunteered.

"Right. And insurance that's beyond the pale. We have regular coverage for fire, liability, and business interruption. But that's nothing compared with what's required by the Dram Act. If you leave here and pile into someone with your car, both you and your victim can sue us for getting you drunk. How's that for justice?"

My friend capitulated. "I give up. You're making me cry, so you owe me a drink."

"Agreed, but not before I've finished. There's also several kinds of taxes, the license fee, depreciation of equipment, and breakage. This crystal has a very short life expectancy. Anyhow, you get the point, it's not just pure profit." I motioned to the bartender. "Another martini, Thatch. Say, that reminds me . . ."

My friend pretended to be horrified. "No, not another expense, I can't take it."

"Still, it exists. It's called 'sticky fingers'."

When the drink arrived, I asked the bartender to stay and meet my friend. "Thatch here started working as second bartender just after we opened. Tell my friend what you learned from the fellow you worked under."

Thatch gave one of his broad Burmese smiles and began. "He show me some tricks how to steal, like you wave bottle around, pour up and down, customer think he's getting extra big drink. Really he get short drink, because bartender counts and knows to the drop what he pours. Bartender then sell extra left in bottle but not ring up on register. Money from customer go right in pocket. Another way, if manager doesn't count empty bottles, is to pour doubles, so to get extra tip. Sometime that bartender he even bring bottle from home and go into business for himself here. He also very sharp with customer checks. He ring up only one or two drink but charge for all drink and put difference in pocket. Sometime he leave register open and not ring up drink at all, but that usually when Dicky not around. He also very good on short change, and twenty dollar bill sometime become ten dollar on way to register. If customer complain, bartender say just a mistake. That bartender tell me he make fifteen or twenty dollar a day extra in different way, more on Saturday night when lots of customers. I don't think he pay income tax on that," he added solemnly.

"So you see," I added my bit, "there's a real Christmas Club here, and most of it right out of the profits."

My friend wasn't really listening, apparently mulling over the implications of Thatch's story. "Say," he suddenly addressed the bartender, "if you know so much about how to cheat the company or the customer, how do we know you're honest?"

Thatch looked at him with an enigmatic smile. "Oh, no reason to worry, sir," he declared, "I not have enough practice yet."

Waiters, too, have their own tricks when it comes to fattening their purses, and for that matter their bodies as well. The cash potential is probably not so good as for bartenders, but there is the added compensation of snacking at the owners' expense. As a class, waiters seem to be congenitally famished, especially for sweets, and on a busy night, when the chef is preoccupied with orders, it is surprising how much simply disappears from a kitchen. They do not care much for bread, nor do they favor soups. Rather, they like pastries, preferably those made with butter, ice cream of all flavors, and fruit, if it is out of season. Imported cheeses, custards, chocolate *mousse* and goodies of that sort have a short life in the cooler if not kept under lock and key. All of these items are good for bone and muscle, which may explain the robustness of so many waiters. On the other hand, the bartender who helps himself too freely from the supplies at hand may end up with cirrhosis.

Admittedly, it is more difficult and risky for the waiter to channel the customers' cash into his pocket than for a bartender. But there are ways. A discreet waiter may often take an order on a small card or pad, so as not to intimidate his clientele with the ominous sight of the dinner check itself. Who, after all, is going to indulge an impulse for a dozen *escargots* or *omelete norvégiène* if he is confronted with the evidence of his extravagance *avant la lettre?* In fact, this same discreet waiter may never offend his customers with the sight of the official dinner check at all, because none exists. Instead, he presents a slip, itemized or otherwise, indicating the amount owed, and if he receives cash it goes directly into his pocket and home. Should you, the customer, at this point produce a diner's credit card, you are guilty of foul play, for it obliges the waiter to then trouble the cashier to punch your entire meal on a register check and fill out the credit slip. The deceived victim of your thoughtlessness must then return to your table, and, masking his disappointment with a genial smile, accept your paltry "gratuity" in lieu of the entire amount for your dinner.

The best way for a restaurant to limit, if not entirely avoid, losses from this artifice is to impose and enforce an edict that nary a morsel be even prepared until the waiter produces a dinner check with the item and its cost posted by the kitchen register. That does reduce losses, but it assumes that the kitchen cashier cross checks every dish leaving the kitchen with the same care as a controller at Fort Knox. Even then there are fissures, for an enterprising waiter can smuggle a chocolate *mousse* under a hot cover or whisk a brace of *éclairs* past even a watchful cashier, especially if they are tidily nested in the corner of a basket of rolls. Such items may be charged to the customer on the slip presented to him, but not rung up on the register. The waiter pockets the difference between the two bills.

Waiters have a habit of losing dinner checks unless they are numbered, with each waiter receiving a recorded sequence which must be accounted for at the evening's end. A missing check is a sure sign that someone has been in business for himself. Fines can be imposed, but the hardened thief will risk the penalty if it is less than the profit. Another strategem, which involves no deductions in the way of fines, is to claim that the customer skipped without paying. Managers seldom run down the street after departed guests to confirm the possibility that a waiter may be lying.

Deceptions such as these are common enough, though their abuse may occasion the necessity of seeking employment elsewhere. *La Garonne* seemed to have an inordinate appeal to customers who left without paying, and dinner checks inexplicably disappeared with alarming frequency. Smuggling food from the kitchen was no problem, if indeed one even had to bother when Nicky was in the slot. But if he did become unaccountably hostile and start checking carefully, it was only necessary to wait until he wanted a cigarette. When he was occupied with that performance, one could have trundled a roast ox past his slot unobserved.

La Garonne had other kinds of thieves among the kitchen help and service personnel who were far less artful than some of our more enterprising bartenders and waiters. These were the simple petty larcenists who pilfered or stole in a haphazard manner without *élan* or ingenuity. When caught, these miserable specimens rationalized their disloyality and dishonesty as retribution for insufficient wages or because "Everyone does it." Although what they stole didn't amount to much on a daily basis, still this uninspired herd played its modest role in helping destroy *La Garonne*.

24

One morning at dawn, André François Dupuis awakened feeling so sick that he called an ambulance to take him to the hospital, where his condition was diagnosed as pneumonia complicated by chronic ailments. Although he was desperately ill, he phoned Rudolph to issue instructions and he also reported his condition to me. When I visited him later that day, he looked ghastly, and by next evening he was delirious and on the critical list. His doctor's question to me about next of kin implied the worst, and I alerted Jack to stand by to handle "arrangements." Incredibly, three days later and against his doctor's vehement protestations, André François Dupuis signed himself out of the hospital. Within a week, he was back at *La Garonne*, if only to call in his orders to purveyors and spend a few hours tottering around the kitchen. He was too stubborn to rest and too sick to work.

For Harry, the chef's absence was a cause for jubilation, and he celebrated with holocausts of cognac and *Grand Marnier*. He also indulged his craving for filet of beef, which the compliant Rudolph broiled for him in defiance of the chef's decree that everyone, himself included, eat only the regular meal prepared for employees. But more important to Harry than the opportunity of satisfying his appetites for pyrotechnics and filet was the possibility of demonstrating to the managerial junta that *La Garonne* could easily do without "that old fart." At every possible occasion, he inferred that the kitchen had never run so well as during Dupuis' absence, and Harry's praise for Rudolph was particularly lavish. The implications of his remarks were clear, as was the nobility of spirit underlying them.

André François Dupuis was not defenseless, and he had sources of information among the waiters, especially those who resented Harry's practice of snagging the best parties for himself. Even before the chef left the hospital, he knew that Harry was eating filet and plotting his downfall. It was the spectre of Harry's triumph that goaded him into throwing off the shroud and returning from the grave. Once back, he set about haunting Harry.

Dupuis knew that the junta was dead set against hiring pansies and that we attributed not a few of *La Garonne's* miseries to the presence of "that element." Therefore, on the next occasion that Harry hired some replacement waiters, the chef relayed to me his suspicion that they were of the undesireable persuasion. Immediate investigation revealed nothing, except it was clear that Harry himself completely agreed with the injunction against hiring such types, however discriminatory that might be. André François Dupuis seemed to have lost his opening.

A few mornings later, the porter called Dwight to report that when he had arrived to begin cleaning he had found overturned chairs, broken glasses, and empty liquor bottles in the main dining room. This was unusual, and he thought someone should know about it. Dwight called me and we met at the restaurant. Our cursory examination pointed to an after-hours revel by some of the employees, a most serious matter because it jeopardized our liquor license. The porter had found the bar locked, so the only other source was the liquor checked out to the kitchen, which was kept under key by the cashier, Nicky. When Thatch arrived shortly before noon, he volunteered the information that in the course of the previous evening, Nicky had come to the bar several times to check out cognac and liqueur for the kitchen, a fact confirmed by the bar requisition book. Dupuis, however, stated that he had ordered nothing at all from the bar stock the previous night. The cashier's liquor cabinet was unlocked and empty. Nicky did not appear for work, nor could he be reached.

Dwight contacted Jack and Eric and we all met at the latter's house. To put it mildly, Eric was intensely angered by what we had to report. He had been an early and outspoken advocate of *Raid*-ing the fruit farm, and his attitude toward the "element" had not improved when we had discovered the order for long-stemmed red roses. Now, learning of Nicky's presumed malfeasance, his wrath made Thor's fury seem a whisper. While he raged about, Jack and I took refuge behind large pieces of furniture, but even there we had no sense of security. The dedicated Dwight, true to his Hippocratic oath, courageously remained exposed and prepared to treat apoplexy.

Eric's huge fists clutched and crushed his imagined victim as he blundered around the room. "Why that dirty little creep! So he thinks he's going to party on our booze, does he? Well, he's gonna get a knuckle sandwich to eat with it. He's mine, he's all mine. I get to kick his ass into the street. That damn creep. 'I'm tho thorry, I promith not to do it again.' I've heard that before. This time you're right, 'cause you won't be able to do it again when I get finished. Let me know the moment he shows. Day or night. I'll be there in ten minutes. Just keep him for ten minutes. I'm gonna fix his wagon good. In fact, he's gonna be missing some wheels!" His words became increasingly black and choked, and their import was clear. Simply to fire Nicky was not enough: he had to suffer some extravagant punishment, one which would, as it were, geld the lily.

But Eric-the-Gelder did not fulfill the menace of his new title. Rather, he spared the blood and foiled the child. In a few days Nicky returned, obviously prepared for the axe — figuratively speaking. Under Eric's lowering gaze, he expressed contrition for his act, and in his confession he implicated a couple of the new waiters who had aroused the chef's suspicions. He was prepared to leave without hard feelings. He wanted only the week's wages owed him and $850 which Dicky had promised for his help during the renovation. Eric thought of his original plan but restrained himself. The answer was brief and blunt. Wages could be discussed when Nicky refunded the several hundred dollars missing from his register. As for the $850, it was a relatively cheap lesson that all contracts should be in writing. Nicky didn't insist, but before he left, he treated himself to a final cigarette. Eric was appalled.

The just-fired Nicky and the recently-fired Dicky were joined by the decorator Micky, and the trio, exhibiting a fine sense of the appropriate, set off for the Virgin Islands, accompanied by a $5,000 electric organ purchased on time by Dicky from a local company which was unaware of his plan for export. As for Dicky's notes at the bank, which once we had so eagerly co-signed, these became our problem. Dicky also abandoned his car to the finance company, whose agent shortly appeared at Jack's office and demanded from him the balance of payments as co-signer of the auto loan. Jack inspected the contract. His name had indeed been signed, but it wasn't his signature.

25

Our junta took its charge most seriously, and we were resolved that even if the white elephant could not be cured, it might at least be kept on its feet and showing signs of life. Try propping up an elephant, particularly one whose legs have become mush and whose ponderous body is racked by convulsive spasms. Only intensive care and emergency underpinning prevented the collapse of the drooping beast, which constantly threatened to crush or suffocate us under its massive but boneless bulk.

Without a manager, it fell our lot to have one of our number present every night to close the restaurant and carry the receipts, such as they were, to the night depository of a nearby bank. At first this task was cheerfully performed. *La Garonne* was, after all, still an elegant place, and on a busy weekend night it acquired a vitality and vibrancy which belied its fatal affliction. At such times one might even be beguiled by momentary thoughts of a possible recovery, and it was not unpleasant to sit anonymously in a dark corner of the bar sipping a drink and conferring occasionally with employees who came to the shadowed table for keys or counsel. Meanwhile, there was the spectacle of the colorful group at the bar to enjoy, and it was often rewarding to eavesdrop on the animated conversations which drifted in from the dining rooms.

As amateur managers we soon discovered, however, that

the night watch, which lasted until 2:00 A.M., did not mesh well with our non-restaurant activities, which began at 8:00 A.M. Highballs provided the stamina to stay awake until closing, but they had the effect of retarding the will to arise betimes the following morning. Very shortly, the duty of closing became a penitential chore, a joyless task endured with grim determination. After midnight the very minutes began to drag, especially in the early part of the week when the dining rooms were empty by eleven o'clock and only a handful of customers remained at the bar. Unlike the weekend celebrants, who brought with them a contagious night-on-the-town atmosphere, the week night drinkers were inclined to moroseness. Hardly more tolerable than the sullen demeanor of the silent majority was the aggressive sociability of the occasional happy drinker, who glued himself to anyone displaying the slightest inclination to listen to his broken-record discourse.

"Say, fella, do you know wha the *four* flavors are? I'll just bet you don't know wha the four flavors are. You know wha I mean? Not flavors like chocolate, but the *four* flavors. There's only four of them, but most people think there's more. You don't know? I didn't think so. Well, here's the four flavors. There's salt, and sweet, and bitter, that's the four flavors. You didn't know that, did you. How did I know you didn't? Because most people don't know. My brother-in-law don't even know, and he went to Ohio State. But there's just those four, like I said, bitter, and sweet, and salt, and the fourth is, yea, bitter. I'll bet this Chink bartender don't know either. Hey, bartender, you know wha the four flavors are? This guy don't know. He don't even know one of them. He thought it was chocolate or something like that. But that's not the four flavors. You know wha I mean?"

Inevitably, one or two die-hards stayed until the last call, and then lingered over their drinks until a taxi finally appeared to haul the remains. Then the registers had to be cleared, the cash counted, deposit slips made out, and the whole place locked up. When the front door closed on the last employee, an ominous silence descended on the cavernous rooms, broken only by the sobbing drains and random knocking in the heating pipes. The checking of locks began in the farthest corner of the basement, the location of the liquor storage rooms, which could be reached either by a perpendicular stairway from behind the bar or through a basement passage whose low ceiling was lined with pipes that reached for the scalps of the unwary, then back along this dark corridor and on to the offices and storerooms. When the store-room lights had been extinguished, there was total darkness, broken only by a faint light from the top of the stairs to the kitchen. At that moment, a compressor might whine into action or the furnace blast off, sending one scurrying for the stairs — and smack into a pipe right along the hairline.

The light panel for the main floor was at the cashier's slot between the kitchen and main dining room. Everything had to be turned off there, plunging the entire place into blackness. The way to the front door was fraught with obstacles, so it was necessary to grope along, feeling with one hand for the chairs and table corners and clutching the deposit bag in the other. A barked shin was par for this course, but then that worked as a counter-irritant for the throbbing forehead. The foyer had some tricky stairs, and these constantly changed their number to increase the difficulty of the obstacle course. The front door was passed with a feeling of relief unjustified by the menace of the deserted streets. At home by the cheery hour of 3:00 A.M. or later, the insomnia which was symptomatic of *La Garonneitis* guaranteed a view of dawn.

We had at first thought to postpone hiring a manager in order to save another $200 a week, but after a month of closing every night we agreed to forego that economy. We had battle fatigue and liver spots, lacerated foreheads, and charcoal circles under red rimmed eyes. We were the incarnation of the restaurant's desperate condition.

26

In our quest for a manager, we knew specifically what we didn't want, that is, another Dicky. We were less certain of what we did want, though there was vague talk about managerial skills, experience, knowledge of accounting procedures, experience with portion control, and habits of a night owl. Flamin' 'Arry proposed himself for the position, but we knew that his appointment would result in André François Dupuis' instant departure. Also, Harry's incendiary propensities were better applied in the dining room than the office, although, in the TOP SECRET drawer of our minds, we filed the pregnant thought that our misery could hardly be worsened if Harry fired up some V.S.O.P. in a remote corner of the basement some night.

Letters were written to prospective managers, and remained unanswered. A few interviews were arranged, but no one seemed suitable. One person appeared reasonably qualified, but his candidacy was instantly terminated when he succumbed to the infectious yawning which racked those of us interviewing him.

Ultimately we found our man in a peppery little French Canadian who had a job somewhere as a night bartender, which suggested at the very least a capacity to stay awake regularly past midnight. Henri, as he was named, was young, but he had ten years' experience in the restaurant business, having started as a dishwasher while virtually a child. He had enthusiasm and dynamism, and he was unawed by our disclosure of *La Garonne's* financial problems. The moment he was hired, we all went to bed.

Henri came on strong. He had enormous self-confidence and more than a little gaul. He knew what he wanted to do and forthrightly outlined his immediate plans to the junta and Jack.

"You fellas," he declared, "don't know your ass. No wonder you're on the skids. You got no cocktail trade and you don't serve lunches. It don't cost a penny more to have the bar full or to use this place at noon. Here's what I'm gonna do. I'm gonna get a girl with a big pair of boobs to tend bar, and we'll serve doubles during the cocktail hour. Those lawyers and bankers downtown'll come like flies. And I'm gonna get some good lookin' broads to serve a businessmen's lunch. And to hell with all that French crap — we'll serve that at dinner."

As far as Henri was concerned, Harry was just another limey waiter, and he quickly put him in his place. Our new manager didn't object to Harry's continuing as dining room captain, but he made him share the best clientele with the other waiters. Harry endured this loss of privilege stoically, but he was unprepared for Henri's next move, the rationing of *Grand Marnier* and cognac. For a week, he tried to accustom himself to the feeble fires provided by a mere double shot, but his heart wasn't in it. If there could be no spectacle, there would be no Harry, and so he quit.

A new broom sweeps clean, and, once Harry was out the door, Henri turned to the kitchen. André François Dupuis had never been moved by a broom in his life, and he wasn't about to accept orders from someone who hadn't even been born when he already ranked among the top in his profession. Henri could do as he liked in the dining room and bar, but the kitchen was the chef's affair. He would choose his purveyors, he would determine the menu, he would hire and fire his staff. As the chef expressed it, "Zat leetle squeak-pip knows nozeeng about zee *cuisine*. Ow kan ee tell me somezeeng?"

Henri brought his problems with Dupuis to our meetings, explaining that profits were impossible unless blue chip purveyors were replaced, the menu revised, an American lunch introduced, and the kitchen payroll further reduced. He recommended that the chef take a cut in salary until such time as profits justified restoring his $400 a week. If the chef didn't like it, Henri knew where another could be found. We had to agree that the pressure of circumstances gave weight to Henri's plans, though obviously the character of the restaurant would change with their implementation. We agonized over the matter for a couple of weeks while Henri harangued us, cajoled us, made promises and threatened to quit if we vetoed his plans. Beggars can't be choosers, and besides, whatever Henri did could hardly cause us to lose money faster than we had lost it before. We decided to stand behind Henri, to give him virtually complete control. For the first time in the enterprise's history, business considerations were put before sentiment.

In France, there is a time honored custom called *lagniappe*, a variation of the kick-back, by which a cook establishes a mutually profitable relationship with various markets, faithfully buying everything from them in exchange for a discount which the cook pockets. This is considered a cook's prerogative, but it is not to be abused. André François Dupuis had a fine sense of tradition, and if in fact he did have an arrangement such as this with his purveyors or their agents, it was doubtless within approved limits. Perhaps his reluctance to change suppliers was connected with this *lagniappe*, or perhaps he felt that Henri, in seeking to force a change to other purveyors selected by himself, was hoping to get kick-backs of his own. In any case, the chef tenaciously held to his right to order from whom he wished, even while agreeing to a nominal reduction in salary. He also acceded to the idea of reopening at noon, although he flatly stated that there would be no profit in serving cheap lunches.

The contest over purveyors came to a showdown. Henri insisted they be changed, and the chef was adamant they wouldn't — he would quit first. Henri found the idea appealing and said he could leave any time. While Henri prepared a terminal check, André François Dupuis went to pour out his sauces, an act which traditionally accompanies the departure of a chef. Our *chef de cuisine* left Huron that night. It was the end of an era at *La Garonne*.

27

We agreed to close the restaurant for a brief interval to give Henri time to find another chef and recruit a staff for the luncheon trade. The chef whom he acquired, although no master, seemed competent to prepare some of the dishes which had appeared on the old menu, and his proposed businessmen's lunch had promise. Best of all, he was $200 a week less than Dupuis and needed only two other cooks beside himself. Henri soon lined up his waitresses, and *La Garonne* was reopened.

For a few weeks, things looked favorable, although the operation still ran in the red. In an effort to stimulate Henri to even greater achievements, we offered him a share of the corporation. His immediate response was enthusiastic, but after conferring with his wife, whom he had hired as hostess and bookkeeper, he declined. At the same time, he insisted on a raise and a week's vacation, which we granted.

When he had first taken over, Henri was confident he could temporize with the creditors and, by operating carefully with the cash receipts, he could meet the salaries, rent, chattel mortgages and so forth, gradually working the corporation out of debt. At the time, this seemed overly optimistic, although we appreciated his good intentions. Now, after a month's exposure to the erosion of our indebtedness, he asked for and got an additional $20,000, which instantly went to cover unescrowed withholding taxes, license renewals, overdue utilities bills, and delinquent contract payments. This bought more time to incur further indebtedess.

Then the house of cards collapsed. Henri's chef got a disabling attack of "long tongue" and took off, never to be heard from again — until he filed for unemployment compensation. The quality of the *cuisine* plummeted, going from *sole veronique* to fish sticks overnight. The faithful Thatch, who had almost become an institution behind our bar, gave notice and left. Simple pilferage gave way to brazen thievery. Exasperated creditors would no longer listen to promises, and Henri had to bar the door with his own person to prevent repossessions. The truth was revealed in flashing neon lights that could not be ignored — *La Garonne* was finished. We made our first smart decision in the restaurant's one year of operation. We locked the doors for good.

What had happened? Some bad luck, some bad apples, but, in retrospect, fatal weaknesses had existed from the beginning. Under-capitalization at the outset had led us to lease rather than build, but we ended up pouring more money into our tumble-down shack than a new building would have cost. Over-optimism blinded us to the fact that since the business had lost money from the day it opened, some drastic kill-or-cure remedy should have been administered in the early months of operation. Our failure to observe the special adage directed at restaurateurs, "Too many cooks spoil the broth," left basic problems unresolved, because our executive decisions were always compromises. Our ignorance of the restaurant business made us pigeons prime for plucking, since we had to believe what we were told — and that means we could believe anything. And no one among the inves-

tors was willing to be at the restaurant to open the doors to employees and close them when they departed, and to stay there
while they worked.

But at the top of list of causes of failure, was our prevailing attitude, even in adversity, that the whole enterprise was a
game, a restaurant variation of MONOPOLY where weekly grosses,
loans, lines of credit, accounts payable, mortgages and rents were
just alternatives dependent upon a roll of dice and represented
by sheaves of play money. Sooner or later a "Chance" card would
turn up to ensure our winning. But while we weren't taking *La
Garonne* seriously, it took us very seriously indeed.

One afternoon shortly after we closed, Jack and I had
reluctantly gone down to the restaurant to complete an inventory
of the kitchen equipment. The whole place was so depressing
and our task so joyless as to affect even Jack's blithe spirit, and
our mood wasn't helped by the loathsome stench of spoiling fish
from one of the freezers. Fractured French seemed an appropriate activity, and we had run through *la même chose* (That's what
I call a *mini*-skirt) and *Je suis fatigué* (I am an obese Swiss homosexual) when the service bell at the back door rang, arousing Jack
to the happy suggestion that maybe someone had come to repossess the seafood. We opened the door to be greeted by a truck
driver, who cheerily presented a wad of invoices and asked where
he should put the delivery. We informed him that the restaurant
was more than temporarily closed. He replied that it was all the
same to him, but someone would have to pay if the delivery were
returned. Wearily we told him to unload it.

The pyramid of cartons contained the final irony. At the
moment when the restaurant had been in its last death agonies,

the frugal Henri had decided to take advantage of discounts offered for quantity orders — and he had contracted for 15,000 dinner checks embossed *La Garonne* and twenty cases of silk textured match books bearing the restaurant's name and phone number.

What do you do with 50,000 match books?

ADVERTISEMENT

If you are considering opening a restaurant, you absolutely need dissuasion by experts. Employing the consultants of *"Restaurant NO!"* will save you untold thousands of dollars, which may then be frittered away on such whims as around the world cruises, private airplanes, vacation houses, and expensive jewelry.

Our contract is as follows: You, the prospective restaurateur, put $2,000.00 into escrow. Our seasoned consultants, Ivan Meursault and Jack Corcoran, will then spend a weekend with you to point out in gruesome detail the folly of your intentions and the naiveté of your plans. If you are brought back to sanity and dissuaded, you pay only the consultants' travel and accommodations. Should you persist in your madness and actually open a restaurant, within one year your books will be inspected. If you can show a profit, you retain the $2,000.00 in escrow. If you show a loss, as unquestionably you will, then $2,000.00 will go to *"Restaurant NO!"*